CLASSIC LITERATURE MADE SIMPLE

JOSEPH PEARCE

Classic Literature
Made Simple

Fifty Great Books in a Nutshell

IGNATIUS PRESS   SAN FRANCISCO

Cover Art:
Vsevolod Mikhailovich Garshin (1855–1888).
1884.
by Ilya Repint (1844–1930)
Oil on canvas, 35 × 27¼ in. (88.9 × 69.2 cm).
Gift of Humanities Fund Inc., 1972 (1972.145.2)
Location: The Metropolitan Museum of Art/New York, NY/USA
© The Metropolitan Museum of Art
Image source: Art Resource, New York

Cover design by Pawel Cetlinski

© 2024 by Ignatius Press, San Francisco
All rights reserved
ISBN 978-1-62164-722-5 (PB)
ISBN 978-1-64229-318-0 (eBook)
Library of Congress Catalogue number 2024938092
Printed in the United States of America ∞

CONTENTS

PREFATORY ACKNOWLEDGMENT

Each of the chapters in this book originally appeared as part of an online series for *Crisis Magazine* (2021–2023) in which the author endeavored to put fifty great books into the idiomatic "nutshell", summarizing their themes and ethical spirit in a thousand words or so.

INTRODUCTION ON THE READING OF GOOD AND BAD BOOKS

It has been said, quite correctly, that we write as well as we read. It can also be said, equally correctly, that we think as well as we read. Since our very thoughts are communicated to ourselves and to others by the use of words, it stands to reason that the better our vocabulary, the better will be our ability to make sense of reality. This is why the Anglo-Saxons spoke of each person possessing his own individual word-hoard. The larger the word-hoard we possess, the richer we are.

Since reading well is so important, it is good to get into the habit of reading good books. The better the book, the better will be our ability to think well and write well. This being so, it is good to be able to judge what constitutes a good book from a bad book.

Generally speaking, there are two types of good books and two types of bad books. A book can be good in the sense that it is well written, and it can also be good in the sense of the morality that it communicates. Conversely, a book can be bad in the sense that it is poorly written and can also be bad in the sense of the morality, or lack thereof, that it conveys. Logically, therefore, we can say that there are four types of books. There are good-good books, bad-good books, good-bad books, and bad-bad books. There are books that are well written and convey good morals; books that are poorly written but convey good morals; books that are well written that are immoral; and books that are poorly written and immoral.

We needn't waste our time on bad-bad books—those which are poorly written and convey a bad moral philosophy. But what of the other types of books?

It goes without saying that good-good books are worth reading, but what of the bad-good books and the good-bad books? The former are poorly written but morally sound. Many self-published works of Christian fiction fall into this category, though by no means all. Should we read them? There is perhaps no moral objection to our doing so, except insofar as we are wasting time that could be better spent reading good-good books.

But what about the good-bad books, which are well written but convey questionable or execrable morals? These are certainly seductive, insofar as we might enjoy their literary merit and even perceive real beauty in the masterful control of plot and character development or the presence of pyrotechnic eloquence. One thinks perhaps of the works of James Joyce, a Meistersinger in terms of his use of words and his mythopoeic power, who nonetheless uses his superlative talents subversively, warring with the faith in which he was raised and casting his priceless pearls before swine. Should such books be read? Should we be comfortable reading great writers whose philosophies grate with a Christian understanding of reality? Should we read James Joyce, for instance? Should we encourage others to do so?

These were questions with which I struggled when teaching literature at the undergraduate level. For years I omitted teaching Joyce because doing so would have meant leaving out a good-good book, which I thought it more important for my students to read and study, in order to make room for a good-bad book. I was prevailed upon to teach Joyce on the basis that any of my students proceeding to graduate school would be seriously disadvantaged if they hadn't read him. I saw the argument but was unconvinced that 90 percent of my students needed to be forced to read a good-bad book instead of a good-good book in order to accommodate the 10 percent who arguably needed to read the former.

Most of us do not need to face such a dilemma. If we can freely choose to read whatever we like, or whatever our conscience dictates, why would we want to read anything but good-good books? Life is too short for us to be able to read all the good-good books that have been written, so why waste our time on anything else?

Christian civilization has given birth to numerous great books as it has given birth to numerous great saints. The former should be canonized as are the latter. Great books, like great saints, enrich our faith as they enrich our culture. As such, reading good books (or specifically good-good books!) should be an integrated part of leading a good life.

I

The Iliad

*Sing, goddess, the anger of Peleus' son Achilleus and its devasta-
tion ... and the will of Zeus [which] was accomplished.*

—Homer, *The Iliad*

The opening lines of Homer's epic, *The Iliad*, say it all.
In these first few words, the poet betrays his purpose and
unpacks the deepest meaning of his work.

He begins with a prayer to his Muse, the goddess of
creativity, requesting the grace he needs to tell the story
well and honestly. In doing so, he is acknowledging that
creativity is a gift of the gods and that without their supernatural help (*grace*) the poet or artist can achieve nothing.
His work is therefore a work of piety, as well as a work
of poetry. He desires to tell the truth and seeks the help of
divine intercession to enable him to do so.

The truth he intends to tell is not factual or historical truth, because he is writing of the stuff of legend and
of events that happened several centuries earlier. He will,
therefore, tell his tale using the poetic license necessary to
tell a good story, weaving fact with fiction into a seamless

The Iliad of Homer, trans. Richmond Lattimore (Chicago: University of Chicago, 1951), bk. 1, lines 1–2, 5.

narrative fabric. No, the truth he means to tell is not historical truth (facts), but *moral* truth. He is going to present to us, in powerful dramatic form, an important moral lesson, holding up the "mirror to man" that, as Tolkien suggested, is one of the main purposes of fairy stories. The moral he is going to present is that anger, the cankered fruit of pride, is destructive and that it has devastating consequences, not merely for Achilles, the prideful man, full of wrath, but for countless other people, the innocent victims of Achilles' sin. Thus, in Robert Fitzgerald's translation, Achilles' "doomed and ruinous" anger "caused the Akhaians loss on bitter loss and crowded brave souls into the undergloom, leaving so many dead men—carrion for dogs and birds" (1.2–6).[1] Sin does not merely harm the sinner; it harms countless others also. Actions have consequences, and bad actions have bad consequences. This is Homer's lesson. It is, however, not his only lesson. We forget, at our peril, that this connection between immoral behavior and destruction is not merely fatalistic but providential. It is, as Homer is at pains to point out, "the will of Zeus [which] was accomplished" (1.5).

As Achilles' rage runs riot, riding roughshod over his reason as much as it rides roughshod over his neighbors (both his friends and enemies), he incurs the wrath of God. In following his own prideful passion for revenge, rather than the path of virtue, Achilles brings down the judgment of Zeus upon himself. His destruction is, therefore, the workings not merely of blind fate but of divine providence.

The theology that underpins Homer's epic is of course pagan. It is intriguing, however, that Homer's polytheism seems to be drifting in a monotheistic direction. The

---

[1] Homer, *The Iliad*, trans. Robert Fitzgerald (Garden City, N.Y.: Anchor Press/Doubleday, 1974). Text references are to book and line.

power of Zeus does not merely exceed the power of all the other gods, taken individually; it exceeds the power of all the other gods combined. When he makes this claim to effective omnipotence to the assembly of gods, none contradicts him. This does not stop the gods conspiring against Zeus' will but, irrespective of such ultimately futile efforts, it is his will and not theirs that comes to pass. There are even hints of Zeus' omniscience when he informs Hera, after she had beguiled him to sleep in the hope of circumventing his will, of all that will happen in the future of the war, his prophetic words becoming reality as the story unfolds. If Zeus knows the future as fact, his knowledge is not constrained by time but transcends it.

Homer waxes metaphorical in the penultimate book of the epic, revealing his overarching moral in the events surrounding the disputed outcome of the chariot race, the resolution of which displays a magnanimity of spirit sorely lacking in the actions of the war. The disputes arising over the alleged immoral actions during the race are analogous to the immoral actions of the key characters in the epic as a whole, the chariot race serving metaphorically as a microcosmic representation of the war itself. The message is clear enough. If Paris, Helen, Agamemnon, Achilles, and others had displayed the same honest and magnanimous spirit as that displayed in the resolution of the disputes after the race, the war could have been avoided and the injustices resolved without the hatred and the bloodshed.

It is curious that *The Iliad* does not end as it had begun with a focus on Achilles and his destructive and ultimately self-destructive anger. This would have been the symmetrically formal way of concluding the epic. The absence of such an expected denouement is evidently due to Homer's wishing to deflate Achilles' pride by ending his epic with a litany of praise for "blameless" Hector. It is the heroism of the innocent victim of the sins of others, of Paris' lustful elopement with Helen and Achilles' hateful anger, who is lionized at the epic's conclusion. Homer does not glorify war, and still less does he glorify the sin that causes war or the pride and anger that fuels it. He glorifies the man of courage, albeit a man who is not without his own flaws and weaknesses, who lays down his life for his wife and family, and for his people.

Such is the moral that Homer teaches. He is not a Christian, and the god he worships is not the Christian God. Yet he believes that his talents as a poet are God-given gifts, and he prays to the giver of the gifts for the grace to use them well. He then employs these gifts to show us that the sins of pride and anger are self-destructive, and destructive of others also, and that such sin will not go unpunished by a god who commands that men live virtuously. He is, therefore, a writer of the highest order that Christians and indeed all men of good will should feel comfortable calling a friend and ally.

2

The Odyssey

As with *The Iliad*, Homer begins *The Odyssey* with a prayer to his Muse, the supernatural spirit of creativity, for the inspiration to tell the story of Odysseus well. He begins by recounting that Odysseus' men "were destroyed by their own wild recklessness" (1.7)[1] and then sets the theological scene for the whole epic in the words of Zeus:

> Oh for shame, how the mortals put the blame on us
> gods, for they say evils come from us, but it is they,
>   rather,
> who by their own recklessness win sorrow beyond
>   what is given.
>
> (1.32–34)

These few words, spoken by the father of gods and men, enunciate the principal theme, played out in the story of Odysseus' delayed homecoming, that actions have consequences and that bad actions have bad consequences. This is the very theme that Homer had already rehearsed in *The Iliad*.

Try as we might to blame God or the gods for the sufferings in our lives, the sobering fact is that most of our

---

[1] *The Odyssey of Homer*, trans. Richmond Lattimore (New York: Harper Perennial Modern Classics, 2007). Text references are to book and line.

suffering is a consequence of our own reckless behavior or the reckless behavior of others. Yet Homer is also aware that some suffering has what might be called "natural causes" and has nothing to do with the actions of people. This suffering is, in the words of Zeus, the sorrow that is "given", the suffering that is, in some sense, a gift. It can be seen, therefore, that *The Odyssey* is a meditation on the mystery of suffering. It is, however, more than that. It is also a meditation on the wisdom to be acquired from the experience of suffering. This is why some suffering or sorrow is given. It enables the suffering soul to grow in wisdom and virtue.

If suffering is the theme of the epic, its form is that of a journey. It is no surprise that the very word "odyssey", inspired by Homer's original epic, has entered the language as a word meaning "journey", especially a journey that is also an adventure or a quest. The journey of Odysseus, his odyssey, is not merely an adventure but a quest to return home. He is delayed by his own recklessness and by that of his men.

Odysseus' original sin is the pridefulness that calls down the curse of Poseidon on him and his men. He had employed his legendary resourcefulness to execute an escape from the clutches of the cyclops, Polyphemus, claiming that his name was "Nobody". After the escape, Odysseus shouts out boastfully to Polyphumus that he was not "Nobody" but was Odysseus of Ithaka. Having left his calling card, Polyphemus calls down the curse of Poseidon on Odysseus and his men. If Odysseus had been content to remain nobody, embracing humility, he and his men would have returned home expeditiously. Similarly, it is the recklessness of his men, who eat the cattle of Helios in defiance of repeated warnings of the consequences of doing so, which leads to their destruction.

Bereft of his men and his ship, Odysseus is washed up on the island of the goddess Kalypso, who offers him immortality if he will marry her. In the face of this very real temptation, Odysseus chooses death in the embrace of his mortality. He also accepts the dangers and suffering inherent in the renewal of his quest to return home to his wife, son, and people. In choosing a mortal life and a mortal middle-aged wife, instead of immortality and marriage to a timelessly young and perennially beautiful goddess, Odysseus exhibits the great self-sacrificial love that is inseparable from humility.

Upon his final arrival at Ithaka, he is told by the goddess Athene that he cannot return in glory but must be disguised as a beggar, enduring the suffering that his penurious appearance will cause him at the hands of the contemptuously prideful suitors who are besieging Penelope, his wife. Such a scenario provides great dramatic irony, the beggar being refused his own food by the uninvited guests who are consuming it in defiance of the will of both his wife and son. On a deeper level, however, it exposes the suitors as being in breach of the sacrosanct law of xenia, mandated by Zeus, which commands the host to show hospitality to the stranger but also, by extension, commands the stranger to respect the hospitality of the host by not abusing it. This law, which is the pagan equivalent of the commandment of Christ that we love our neighbor, is broken by the suitors in their arrogant abuse of the beggar but also in their contempt of Penelope and Telemachus, their powerless hosts. It is no wonder that Zeus, who is known as the guest's god, will punish such recklessness.

Apart from Odysseus' growth in wisdom and virtue, through the experience of suffering, The Odyssey also shows us a similar path of virtue on the part of his wife and son.

The rite of passage of Telemachus, from boyhood to manhood, is the epic's subplot. At the outset, he is seen to be exasperated at the unwanted and uninvited presence of the suitors, and he is desirous of protecting his mother from their unwelcome advances. He is, however, powerless. His childish frustration is shown in the manner in which he throws down the scepter, the symbol of the authority he cannot wield, in "a stormburst of tears" (2.81). Having gone on his own odyssey, voyaging to the palace of Menelaus in the quest to discover news of his father, he returns home both wiser and stronger. At the end of the epic, he has the physical strength to string his father's bow, indicating that he is now stronger than the suitors who are unable to do so, but also the humility to desist from showing his strength by doing so, refraining at the last moment in obedience to a signal from his father. He has grown, therefore, both physically and morally. He has become a man in the fullest sense of the word.

Last but not least, by any means, is Penelope, whose very presence has understated power and whose voice is that of indomitable virtue. As unbending in fidelity to the gods as she is unbroken in her love for her husband, she is an icon of strong and irrepressible femininity, standing shoulder to shoulder with the greatest of literary heroines, equal in stature to Dante's Beatrice or to Shakespeare's Portia and Cordelia. It is no wonder that the soul of Agamemnon, who had been murdered by his own treacherous wife, should be in awe at the "great virtue [in] the heart of blameless Penelope", proclaiming that "the fame of her virtue shall never die away [because] the immortals will make for the people of earth a thing of grace in the song for prudent Penelope" (24.194–98).

3

Antigone

Sophocles is probably the greatest dramatist in the history of civilization, with the obvious exception of Shakespeare. He lived for ninety years, his life spanning almost the entirety of the fifth century B.C., from 496 to circa 406. During his long life, which seems to have been spent entirely in Athens, he witnessed both the rise and the fall of the Athenian Empire, a period of great social upheaval and political turmoil. He is best known for the Oedipus Cycle, also known as the three Theban plays: *Antigone*, *Oedipus Rex*, and *Oedipus at Colonus*. There are two ways of reading this cycle of plays. They can either be read in their order of composition, as listed above, or in the order of the chronology of the story they tell. *Oedipus Rex* tells of the rise and fall of Oedipus, king of Thebes; *Oedipus at Colonus* tells of Oedipus' old age and death; *Antigone* takes up the story of Antigone, Oedipus' daughter. The advantage of reading them in the order of composition is that we see the growth of wisdom of the playwright reflected in his work: *Antigone* is full of the vigor and vibrancy of political idealism; *Oedipus Rex* is a mature reflection on the mystery and meaning of suffering; *Oedipus at Colonus* takes the reflection on suffering to deeper levels of understanding, answering the questions that *Oedipus Rex* asks. *Oedipus at Colonus*, which was written when Sophocles

was a very old man and was not performed until after his
death, reflects the wisdom of the playwright's ninety years
of accumulated and philosophically digested experience.
We will discuss *Oedipus Rex* and *Oedipus at Colonus* in the
next two chapters. Now, however, we will endeavor to
put *Antigone* in a nutshell.

The play begins as the dust settles on a battle in which
the sons of Oedipus fight on opposing sides and kill each
other in combat. Creon, king of Thebes, declares that one
of the brothers, Eteocles, should be buried with full mil-
itary honors, but that the other, Polynices, is a traitor to
the state who must not be dignified with burial. On the
contrary, Polynices is to be left to rot where he fell, food
for the vultures and the wild dogs. The decision of Antigone, the sister of both deceased warriors, to give her
brother a dignified religious burial in defiance of the law of
the state sets up a drama in which timeless legal and moral
principles are evoked. Does the state have the authority
to deny anyone a dignified burial according to the rites
of religion? Is the power of the state "under God" or is it
a law unto itself? How should those with religious faith
respond to anti-religious laws? How should the state deal
with religious dissidents who disobey its laws?

Forced to choose between the rites and rights of religion and the law of the land, Antigone chooses to be
obedient to the gods in defiance of the law. Her logic is
theological. Creon's law forbidding a religious burial for
her brother is "an outrage to the gods" (88).[1] Seeing reality in terms of her eternal destiny, she fears offending the
gods more than she fears the power of the state to execute
her for breaking its laws. "I have longer to please the dead
than please the living here", she says. "In the kingdom

---

[1] Sophocles, *Antigone*, trans. Robert Fagles (New York, NY: Penguin
Books, 1984). Text references are to line numbers.

down below I'll lie forever" (89–90). Faced with a choice between obeying temporal mortal laws or eternal laws, she proclaims that she will not "dishonour the laws the gods hold in honour" (91–92).

Against Antigone's religious perspective is the secularism of Creon, who declares that "whoever places a friend above the good of his own country is nothing" (203–4). Love of country and obedience to the state trump the love of neighbor.

In the midst of this epic struggle between two opposing worldviews, the religious and the secular, the Chorus, representing the people as a whole, is sympathetic to Antigone but fearful of expressing its dissent in the face of the power of the state. The silent majority is silenced by fear. Antigone tells Creon that the members of the Chorus would praise her for her stance "if their lips weren't locked in fear" (565). It is only through fear of the tyrannical state that the people "keep their tongues in leash" (570).

The plot thickens when we discover that Haemon, Creon's son, is betrothed to be married to Antigone. Haemon tries to reason with his father, reminding him that "only the gods endow a man with reason, the finest of all their gifts, a treasure" (764–65). He also echoes the words of Antigone when he tells Creon that the silent majority is on Antigone's side and that they are only silent through fear:

> The man in the street ... dreads your glance,
> he'd never say anything displeasing to your face.
> But it's for me to catch the murmurs in the dark,
> the way the city mourns for this young girl.
> "No woman," they say, "ever deserved death less,
> and such a brutal death for such a glorious action. . . .
> Death? She deserves a glowing crown of gold!"
> So they say, and the rumour spreads in secret,
> darkly.
>
> (773–84)

Creon, blinded by his own prideful arrogance, is unwilling to see reason, even when the blind prophet Tiresias warns him of the dire punishment from the gods that awaits him if he remains obstinate in his war on the religious rights of the living and the dead. Reiterating the motif of Homer's epics, Sophocles shows us in the tragic consequences of Creon's obstinacy that pride precedes a fall. This moral is driven home unequivocally in the play's final lines, spoken by the Chorus:

> Wisdom is by far the greatest part of joy,
> and reverence toward the gods must be safeguarded.
> The mighty words of the proud are paid in full
> with mighty blows of fate, and at long last
> those blows will teach us wisdom.
>
> (1466–70)

4

Oedipus Rex

Oedipus Rex by Sophocles is more than merely a tragedy. It is a profound meditation on the relationship between fate and free will and on the consequences of that relationship with respect to the mystery and meaning of human suffering. Its plot is convoluted and provocative. Oedipus becomes king of Thebes, after answering the riddle of the Sphynx. Earlier he had unwittingly killed his own father, Laius, and equally unwittingly married his own mother, Jocasta, having several children by her, including Antigone, the eponymous heroine of the play by Sophocles that we discussed above. After Oedipus discovers the full horror of his situation, he stabs himself in both eyes, blinding himself in a fit of madness. The play ends with his clinging to his two young daughters, Antigone and Ismene, before being forcibly separated from them.

The moral of the play is framed by the riddle of the Sphynx: "What goes on four feet in the morning, two feet at noon, and three feet in the evening?" The answer is "man", who crawls as an infant and hobbles with the help of a stick in old age. The riddle serves, therefore, as an aphoristic portrayal of man himself, whose life begins and ends in weakness and utter dependence on others, with an interlude of seeming strength in between. The riddle provides what might be called the *ecce homo* symbolic epigraph, enabling Sophocles to present the axiomatic truth of man's pathetic weakness as the core of the tragedy. *Behold man!*

Oedipus is the man who not only answers the riddle but is himself the answer to it. As we discover in the play's denouement, he was utterly helpless as a baby and was left to die by those responsible for caring for him; he comes of age as king of Thebes and then is doomed to being utterly dependent on others following his act of self-mutilation. As the answer to the riddle, he becomes not merely the tragic figure of one man doomed by circumstance but a representative of Everyman who is similarly doomed. In this sense, at least in some sense, Oedipus is us. The lessons he learns are applicable to all of us.

Apart from the riddle of the Sphinx that frames it, *Oedipus Rex* is itself a riddle, or a series of riddles. To what extent is Oedipus ignorant of the crimes he commits and the taboos he breaks? To what extent does his ignorance signify his innocence? To what extent is life governed by fate? Does fate nullify the reality of human freedom? If everything is governed by fate, is free will illusory or, if not illusory, futile? And if free will is illusory or futile, can humans be held responsible for their actions?

The riddles continue. If Oedipus can be held blameless with respect to his ignorance or with respect to the evil done to him when he was a helpless child, is he not blameworthy for his hubris, especially in his rage-driven attacks on the blind prophet Tiresias? And even if Oedipus, like King Lear, is more sinned against than sinning, what of his father and mother, Laius and Jocasta, who freely chose to leave their child to die in the mountains, or be eaten by wild beasts? Does the blindness of fate exonerate them?

What of the helpless children? What of Antigone and Ismene? How can they be blamed? How can they be considered anything but innocent victims? And where are the gods? Are they present or absent? How can they permit this monstrous fate to play itself out? How can they be free from blame?

And what of ignorance? Can it be bliss? Would it have been better if Oedipus had never asked the questions that led to the horrific revelations and their even more horrific consequences? If it would have been better, as Tiresias says, for Oedipus to remain ignorant of the truth, why did the gods send a plague upon the people of Thebes for the failure to bring Laius' killer to justice?

If Laius and Jocasta received their just deserts for their intention of killing their own infant son, can we be comfortable with the price that the innocent son has to pay for such justice to be done? Isn't Oedipus' fate the adding of insult to injury?

As the foregoing illustrates, *Oedipus Rex* begins with the answering of one riddle and ends with the posing of many others, none of which appears to be answered. It is for this reason that *Oedipus Rex* is so often taught in the (post) modern academy as exemplifying the meaninglessness of life. Life is senseless. It makes no sense. It's all meaningless suffering and nothing else. It's nothing but endless riddles to which there are no answers. As we shall see, however, Sophocles offers answers to all the riddles that he poses in *Oedipus Rex* in the play that is its sequel, *Oedipus at Colonus*, which will be the next great work to be discussed "in a nutshell".

5

Oedipus at Colonus

As we saw in the previous chapter, *Oedipus Rex* presents the riddle of man without offering any solution. It seems to beg innumerable questions on the nature of man and on the mystery of suffering without giving any answers. It would, however, be a gross and grotesque error to conclude from the moral inconclusiveness of *Oedipus Rex* that Sophocles lacked the answers to the questions he poses in the second of his three Theban plays. In the final play, *Oedipus at Colonus*, he solves the riddle of man and the mystery of suffering through the moral lessons that Oedipus has learned from the tragic experiences recounted in the earlier play.

Oedipus at Colonus begins several years after the tragic events that brought down the curtain on *Oedipus Rex*. Oedipus is a broken, blind old man, clad in filthy rags. He is led by his daughter, Antigone, who had been a child at the conclusion of the previous play but is now a young woman.

In his opening speech, Oedipus answers the riddle that the previous play had presented. He reminds Antigone that "acceptance is the great lesson that suffering teaches", explaining that the fruit of such acceptance is "nobility"

(6).[1] These words of wisdom, rooted in the humble acceptance of his plight, set the tone and theme for all that follows.

Like King Lear, Oedipus is a man more sinned against than sinning and, like Lear, he is ennobled by the acceptance of circumstances that were beyond his control and for which he was, therefore, not to blame. He had killed Laius, the man whom he later discovered to be his father, in self-defense. As for Jocasta, the woman he married oblivious of the fact that she was his mother, she and Laius had wanted to destroy him, their own son, in infancy. Whereas they could be said to be responsible for their own tragic ends, Oedipus was an innocent victim of circumstance. As a blameless victim, Oedipus comes to Colonus in the kingdom of Athens as a gift of the gods, "someone sacred, someone filled with piety and power, bearing a great gift for all your people" (312–14).

If Oedipus has become holy through the embrace of his own suffering and is sanctified by his bearing of it, Antigone has also been blessed by her voluntarily laying down her life in her father's service. As Oedipus says, she had "volunteered for grief" (377) ever since leaving childhood behind and coming into fullness of strength. She had wandered with her father, serving as Oedipus' guide, sharing his penury and hunger, cutting her feet walking barefoot over thorny ground, "worn down by the drenching rains, the scorching sun at noon" (380–81). "You endured it all," he tells her, "never a second thought for home, a decent life, so long as your father had some care and comfort" (382–84).

Oedipus also offers a corrective to the suicidal rage that had characterized his act of self-violence in the final moments of the previous play:

---

[1] Sophocles, *The Three Theban Plays: Antigone, Oedipus the King, Oedipus at Colonus* (New York: Penguin Books, 1984). Text references are to line numbers.

That first day, true, when all my rage was seething,
my dearest wish was death.

(483–84)

But then, as "the smoldering fever broke and died at last"
(487), he had come to realize that his rage had far out-
run his wrongs. "I'd lashed myself too much for what I'd
done" (489). He had wished at this point to rebuild his life
as a father to his children but had been forcibly separated
from them and cast into exile. He had learned to accept his
life of wandering poverty, his suffering "received as a gift,
a prize to break the heart" (605).

Theseus, king of Athens, is introduced in a noble light,
made manifest in the charity with which he welcomes
Oedipus:

> I will never shrink
> from a stranger, lost as you are now,
> or fail to lend a hand and save a life.
> I am only a man, well I know,
> And I have no more power over tomorrow,
> Oedipus, than you.
> "Oh Theseus," Oedipus responds, "so magnanimous,
>   so noble!"

(636–42)

It is at this stage in the drama that the supernatural
dimension becomes increasingly apparent. Oedipus tells
Theseus that his magnanimity and charity will be rewarded
by the gods:

> I come with a gift for you,
> my own shattered body ... no feast for the eyes,
> but the gains it holds are greater than great beauty.

(649–51)

When Theseus asks him when the gifts will come to light, Oedipus replies that they will be given after Oedipus' death. Shortly afterward, Oedipus reminds Theseus that only the gods never age and that only the gods never die. "All else in the world almighty Time obliterates, crushes all to nothing" (687–89). The strength of the earth and the strength of men wastes away and dies.

Creon, king of Thebes and Oedipus' brother-in-law, is filled with disgust and contempt upon seeing Oedipus and Antigone in their penurious state, in stark contrast to Theseus' charitable response upon first seeing them. Creon sees Antigone as being foolish for her act of self-sacrifice in helping her father, crushed by the life of gloom and poverty she had chosen. Beyond any prospect of a good marriage, Antigone is fit only for coupling with the most uncouth of men, "a prize for the first rough hand" (853–54) who will take her. He has no inkling of the serenity that Oedipus and Antigone had gained from their willing embrace of suffering. "Our life is not a pitiful as you'd think," Oedipus tells him, "so long as we can find joy in every hour" (911).

Creon, blinded by his pride and the cynicism that is its cankered fruit, has no idea of the peace that passeth understanding of which Oedipus speaks. Theseus, however, sees Oedipus as a prophet who sees more in his blindness than Creon can see with his unblemished eyes. Unlike the contempt with which the blind prophet Tiresias had been treated in the two previous plays, Theseus heeds Oedipus' words:

> Oh I believe you.
> Time and again I've seen your prophecies come right,
> you never lie. Now tell me what to do.
>
> (714–16)

Whereas Creon (in *Antigone*) and Oedipus (in *Oedipus Rex*) were punished by the gods for their dismissal of the blind prophet, Theseus is rewarded for his faith and trust in the gods with a vision of Oedipus being assumed into heaven at the play's literally heavenly climax. The theology of this mystical assumption speaks for itself. The man who accepts the suffering that life brings, embracing it with resignation to the will of the gods, will receive his heavenly reward. It is for this reason that the Chorus, in the play's final lines, beseeches Oedipus' daughters, Antigone and Ismene, to take comfort from their father's miraculous end.

> Come, my children, weep no more,
> raise the dirge no longer. All rests
> in the hands of a mighty power.
>
> (1999–2001)

6

The Aeneid

Along with *The Iliad* and *The Odyssey*, *The Aeneid* is one of the three epic pillars on which the edifice of Western literature rests. These three works are, therefore, foundational.

Written by Virgil a few decades before the birth of Christ, and at least seven centuries after the time of Homer, *The Aeneid* owes its very existence to Homer's earlier epics. It takes its inspiration from an episode in Book 20 of *The Iliad* in which the Trojan warrior Aeneas is saved from death at the hands of Achilles by the intervention of the gods. He is spared so that the Trojan line might not be extinguished, Poseidon declaring to the other gods that it is destined that "Aeneas and his heirs, and theirs, will be the lords of Trojans born hereafter." Virgil takes this divine prophecy and imagines that Aeneas and his heirs would not only prosper but would be destined to found the mighty empire of Rome, rising phoenix-like from the ashes of Troy to rule over their erstwhile Greek conquerors. This militaristic and triumphalist spirit informs the whole epic, which is, at root, an imperialistic celebration of the martial prowess of Rome.

Whereas Homer had begun *The Iliad* by asking his Muse to help him sing of Achilles and the destructive consequences of Achilles' anger, in the light of the will of Zeus that is accomplished through these providential consequences, Virgil proclaims merely that "I sing of warfare and a man of war" (1.1).[1] Flying the Roman imperial flag, Virgil demonizes the Greeks in his retelling of the story of the fall of Troy. We are told that they are not the equal of the Trojans in battle and that they could win the victory only through lies and deception. It is to Virgil that we owe the adage "Beware of Greeks bearing gifts" (2.68–70), an allusion to the treachery of the Trojan Horse. Odysseus, the hero of Homer's epic, becomes, as Ulysses, a villain in Virgil's revisionist account of the siege of Troy and its aftermath.

In spite of his militaristic and patriot predilections, Virgil is the equal of Homer in the tenderness with which he depicts familial love. His description of Aeneas carrying his elderly father, while taking his young son's hand, with his wife beside him, as they endeavor to escape from Troy, is an iconic image of family life, reminiscent of Homer's depiction of Hektor with his wife and son in *The Iliad*. A similar tenderness and sense of empathy is evident in Virgil's telling of the story of Aeneas and Dido, "prisoners of lust" (4.265) who are so besotted with each other that they are utterly negligent of their duty to their respective peoples. It takes direct divine intervention to bring Aeneas to his senses, reminding him of the necessity of putting conscientious duty before unconscionable desire. Virgil's metaphorical employment of an oak tree to embody the immovable and indomitable will of Aeneas to withstand the winds of passion exemplifies Virgil's poetic genius. Dido, on the other hand, fails to govern her own passions, her love for Aeneas turning to hatred, itself a metaphorical prophesy of the Punic Wars between the

---

[1] Virgil, *The Aeneid*, trans. Robert Fitzgerald (New York: Vintage Classics, 1990). Text references are to book and line.

Rome that Aeneas is destined to found and the Carthage of which Dido is queen.

If Virgil's heartrending treatment of the lust-love affair between Aeneas and Dido exhibits the presence of what might be termed a proto-romanticism in the midst of the classical epic, it should not distract us from the poet's primary and epic purpose of leading us to Rome, to which all the threads of the plot are ultimately leading, woven by divine design.

Theologically, Virgil's portrayal of Aeneas' visit to the underworld is rich with theological significance and is more colorful and textured than Homer's portrayal in *The Odyssey* of Odysseus' descent to the dead. In Virgil's epic, the judgment of the dead, and the contrast between the hell of Tartarus and the heaven of Elysium, is far more congruent with the Christian eschatological vision than is the relatively shallow shadowland depicted by Homer. It is no wonder that Virgil's rich vision of the life hereafter should have proved so seminal to the imagination of Dante.

Philosophically, Virgil shows himself to be a follower of Plato in the platonic discourse that he places on the lips of the shade of Anchises, Aeneas' recently deceased father, in the underworld. There are also hints of what might be called purgatory in Anchises' explanation that souls after death "undergo the discipline of punishments and pay in penance for past sins" (6.994–96), adding that "the stain of wrong is washed by floods or burned away by fire" (6.997–98). Ultimately, however, Anchises' discourse leads us back to "illustrious Rome [which] will bound her power with earth, her spirit with Olympus" (6.1048–49). It is to the founding of this "eternal" city, that Virgil is leading us, but he never finally gets us there, the work being unfinished at the time of his death in 19 B.C. This is frustrating, to be sure, leaving us with unanswered and unanswerable questions. For this reason, if for no other, Virgil's epic is not the equal of either of the Homeric pillars with which it stands and to which it owes its very being. The irony is that *The Aeneid* would not have been possible, or even thinkable, if Homer the Greek hadn't been the bearer of the great gifts of *The Iliad* and *The Odyssey*. Let's be thankful, therefore, for Greeks bearing gifts.

7

Beowulf

Beowulf, the Old English epic, probably dates from the early eighth century, a golden age of English Christianity when the land was awash with saints. The *Beowulf* poet, who was almost certainly a monk, was a contemporary of St. Bede the Venerable, a Doctor of the Church, and St. Boniface, the English apostle of the Germans. He was also writing at a time when Anglo-Saxon literature was flourishing. Caedmon, the poet who probably wrote the mystical masterpiece "The Dream of the Rood", had died in 680, a generation or so earlier. It is odd, therefore, that contemporary critics, betraying the arrogance of their ignorance, claim that *Beowulf* is not a Christian poem.

Harold Bloom, exposing his inability to read the allegorical dimension of the poem, claims that "*Beowulf* eschews any mention of Jesus Christ, and all its biblical references are to the Old Testament", adding that the virtues of the poem's eponymous hero "have nothing to do with salvation, and everything to do with warlike courage".[1] He concludes his woefully awry reading of the poem with the preposterous claim that the monk who wrote the poem was a closet pagan: "But does *Beowulf* conclude with the

---

[1] Harold Bloom, introduction to *Bloom's Reviews: Comprehensive Research and Study Guides: Beowulf* (Broomall, PA: Chelsea House Publishers, 1999), 5.

triumph of the Christian vision? God's glory as a creator is extolled in the poem, but nowhere are we told of God's grace. Instead, there are tributes, despairing but firm, to fate, hardly a Christian power."[2]

A reading of the poem from the perspective of the profoundly Catholic culture in which it was written will illustrate, contrary to Professor Bloom's assertions, that there are distinct allegorical references to Christ, especially with respect to His Passion, and that the whole poem has everything to do with salvation in a specifically orthodox theological sense.

Let's begin with the notion that the poet speaks of "fate" in the pagan fatalistic sense. The word that Professor Bloom mistakenly translates as "fate" is the Old English *wyrd*, from which the modern word "weird" is derived. This word, as used in the staunchly Catholic culture of Anglo-Saxon England, meant the mystical presence of divine providence. The idea of the weird-woven web is that all human actions impact others in the communal web in a way that renders the one who acts morally responsible for his actions and answerable to God for them, all of which is subject to, and inseparable from, the "weirdness" of God's providential design. A misunderstanding of the "weirdness" of the poem is, therefore, fatal to any true critical appreciation of it.

Structurally, the poem is divided sequentially by Beowulf's fighting with three monsters: Grendel, Grendel's Mother, and the dragon. The battle against the first two monsters is a parable of the necessity of God's grace and the consequent rebuttal of the heresy of Pelagianism, which was rife in England at the time, as is evident from Bede's *Ecclesiastical History of the English People*, written at around the same time as *Beowulf*. Like Bede, the *Beowulf* poet is warning against the dangers of this heresy which

[2] Ibid., 6.

taught that men could go to heaven by the power of their own will, by merely doing what the Bible teaches, and that, therefore, they did not need the supernatural assistance that theologians call grace.

Let's investigate this parabolic dimension of the poem.

The poet begins by telling us that Beowulf is the mightiest warrior in the world. He can defeat any foe by the brute power of his own strength. He proves as much by spurning all weapons and defeating Grendel through the strength of his own mighty arm. Beowulf seems to epitomize the Pelagian Man, who can defeat evil through the power of his own will and strength without the necessity of any outside assistance, natural or supernatural. He then faces Grendel's Mother, this time carrying the most powerful sword known to man. The sword proves to be powerless against the supernatural power of this new monster, as does Beowulf's own strength. He would most certainly have been killed had not a magical sword miraculously appeared within his grasp. It is through this supernatural assistance that Beowulf prevails, without which he would have perished. "If God had not helped me," Beowulf says, "the outcome would have been quick and fatal."[3] As for the supernatural sword, we discover that its hilt is engraved with biblical images of God's defeat of evil in salvation history. The moral and theological message is clear enough. No human person, however strong, can defeat the power of evil without supernatural assistance (grace), nor can the most powerful works of human ingenuity (the sword signifying what we would now call technology) save us from evil. Our triumph over evil is possible only with divine assistance.

This brings us to the final section in which Beowulf, as an old man, faces the dragon. In this section, numerical

[3] Seamus Heaney, trans., *Beowulf: A New Verse Translation* (New York: W. W. Norton, 2000), 115.

allegorical signifiers are employed to connect Beowulf's fight with the dragon with the Passion of Christ. We are told that Beowulf selected twelve "hand-picked" companions, one of whom was the thief who had raised the dragon's wrath through the stealing of the "precious cup" from the dragon's horde. On the eve of the battle with the dragon, Beowulf is "sad at heart, unsettled yet ready, sensing his death".[4] At the key moment, when Beowulf goes to face the dragon, eleven of his hand-picked followers "broke ranks and ran for their lives to the safety of the wood".[5] Only one of the twelve had the courage to remain by his Lord's side. After Beowulf is slain in his slaying of the dragon, his hand-picked company come skulking from the woods to join the one who had remained at the Lord's side, but only ten of them; the eleventh, the Judas figure, is not with them.

At the poem's conclusion, the people erect a huge burial mound for Beowulf on a headland, "high and imposing, a marker that sailors could see from far away".[6] Then we are told that *twelve* warriors ride around the tomb, mourning the loss of Beowulf as both a man and a king. The traitor, the Judas-figure among the hand-picked troop, has evidently been replaced. The twelve are clearly signifiers of the apostles, which makes Beowulf, in the final part of the poem, in some limited but very real allegorical sense, a Christ figure.

This, in a nutshell, is proof that *Beowulf* is a deeply Christian poem and proof, also, that there are none so blind as critics who will not see the Christian significance of a poem even when it is staring them in the face.

[4] Ibid., 165.
[5] Ibid., 175.
[6] Ibid., 213.

8

The Divine Comedy

The Divine Comedy is arguably the greatest poem ever written. It is also profoundly Catholic to its theological and philosophical core. Its author, Dante Alighieri, spent over ten years writing it, completing it a year before his death in 1321. It is fitting, therefore, that we should celebrate this finest of poetic masterpieces only a few years after the seven hundredth anniversary of the death of its illustrious composer.

Dante was an avid disciple of the Angelic Doctor, St. Thomas Aquinas, the preeminent of all Catholic theologians and philosophers, and it is no surprise, therefore, that St. Thomas' theological and philosophical presence animates the poem from start to finish.

The poem is narrated in the first person by Dante himself, who appears, as it were, as a character in his own imaginative work. It serves as a memento mori, a reminder of death, prompting the poet and his readers to contemplate the Four Last Things: death, judgment, heaven, and hell. The *Comedy* begins, symbolically, on Maundy Thursday, the night on which Christ suffered His Agony in the Garden, with the poet trapped in the dark wood, in the midst of what might now be called a midlife crisis. He is unable to escape because of his slavery to sinful habits and is rescued by the ghost of Virgil, who has been sent through the intercession of the Blessed Virgin and through the agency of St. Lucy, patron saint of the blind, and Dante's beloved Beatrice. In one important sense, Beatrice, the woman whom Dante loved and whose early death devastated him, is the spiritual litmus test by which Dante's progress can be measured. His spiritual ascent is accompanied by the purification of his love for her.

Virgil leads Dante into the depths of hell on Good Friday morning, enabling him to see the horrific consequences of unrepented sin. As they descend deeper and deeper, passing through circles of hell in which each of the seven deadly sins is punished, Dante gains a deeper knowledge of the hatefulness of sin, ending at last in the very pit of hell, in the presence of Satan himself, who is trapped miserably in a sea of ice, ravenously and insatiably famished, devouring the damned souls of the worst of prideful traitors for all eternity. Symbolically, Dante places Satan at the center of the earth, the furthest "down" that anyone can fall, reminding us perhaps of Chesterton's quip that angels can fly because they take themselves lightly, whereas the devil falls by the force of his own gravity.

Having hit rock bottom, Virgil and Dante climb upward toward the distant light, emerging at the foot of Mount Purgatory on Easter Sunday morning. Like the Lord Himself and by His power, they have risen from the dead into the land of the living.

Dante reminds us that purgatory is the antechamber of heaven, the place of cleansing for those already saved, by placing St. Peter's Gate at its entrance. Guarded by an angel, not by St. Peter, who is with the Lord in paradise, the gate is approached by ascending three steps. The first is made of white marble, which is polished to such a gloss that Dante can see his own reflection in it, signifying confession. The second is black and cracked both lengthways and across, so that the cracks intersect, forming the shape of a cross, signifying contrition. The third is as red as blood, signifying satisfaction. The symbolism continues when the angel makes the mark of seven P's upon Dante's brow, signifying the seven deadly sins (the "P" standing for *peccatum*, the Latin word for sin). Each of these P's is removed as Dante ascends through the various parts of the mountain in which each of the seven deadly sins is purged. Finally at the summit of Mount Purgatory, Dante finds himself in the Earthly Paradise, the prelapsarian Eden, the place of primal innocence in which there is no stain of sin. It is here that Dante finally meets Beatrice, and it is here that Virgil takes his leave, the latter being unable to take Dante to paradise.

Beatrice leads Dante into the heavens, symbolized by the planets and the stars, where he meets many saints. St. Thomas Aquinas emerges as the spokesman of the wise, singing the praises of St. Francis and his Lady Poverty, and St. Bonaventure comes forward to praise St. Dominic. In this way, by getting a Dominican to praise St. Francis, and a Franciscan to praise St. Dominic, Dante pours gentle scorn on the tensions between the Dominican and Franciscan orders that existed in his day. In heaven, Dante is telling us, all such worldly differences will be transfigured by perfect love.

Moving further up and further in, Dante meets the apostles and is examined by St. Peter in the virtue of faith, by St. James in the virtue of hope, and by St. John in the virtue of love. His love for Beatrice is purified in a heavenly consummation, each loving the other in their being mutually consumed in the love of God. Moving toward its celestial climax, Dante finally beholds the beauty of the Blessed Virgin and is transported by St. Bernard's prayer of praise to her. The poet's ecstasy is brought to fulfillment in the Beatific Vision itself, shining forth in triune and incarnate splendor, culminating in the poem's final lines in homage to the love that moves the stars.

Maurice Baring, one of the most cultured and well-read men of the last century, summarized the brilliance of Dante's ecstatic conclusion to *The Divine Comedy*:

> Scaling the circles of the *Paradiso*, we are conscious the whole time of an ascent not only in the quality of the substance but in that of the form. It is a long perpetual crescendo, increasing in beauty until the final consummation in the very last line. Somebody once defined an artist ... as a man who knows how to finish things. If this definition is true—and I think it is—then Dante was the greatest artist who ever lived. His final canto is the best, and it depends on and completes the beginning.[1]

Echoing Baring, T. S. Eliot remarked that he was so in awe of Dante's brilliance that he felt that there was nothing to do in his presence but to point to him and remain silent. Thus does the greatest poet of the twentieth century pay homage to the greatest poet of all time. Nothing else needs to be said.

---

[1] Maurice Baring, *Have You Anything to Declare?* (London: William Heinemann Ltd., 1936), 106.

9

The Canterbury Tales

The backdrop to *The Canterbury Tales* by Geoffrey Chaucer is a pilgrimage to the shrine of St. Thomas Beckett, one of the most popular pilgrim sites in the whole of Christendom until its destruction by Henry VIII. It consists of a General Prologue, in which Chaucer introduces the fictional characters who are traveling together on the pilgrimage, and a number of tales told by some of these characters. A very ambitious work, it was unfinished at the time of Chaucer's death in 1400. Although, therefore, we have only fragments of a much bigger work, the fragments are themselves finished tales, told by the various pilgrims.

The General Prologue begins with an evocation of resurrected life. It is April, and sweet showers help to bring new life to every wood and field. This sets the scene for the resurrected spirit of people longing to go on pilgrimage. One such group of pilgrims meet by chance at an inn in London and decide to journey together to Canterbury, telling each other stories along the way. We are then introduced to the pilgrims themselves who are a motley group, comprised mostly of reprobates who are evidently in need of the grace that a pilgrimage brings. There is the Knight, a man of courage and martial prowess who joins the pilgrimage as an act of thanksgiving, having returned from the wars; there is the Knight's son, the Squire, who has the courage of his father in battle but is altogether a dandy in times of peace, wearing the most fashionable clothes and hairstyle and delighting in music and dance. There is the less than holy Prioress, who is vain and fastidious, seeking the pleasures that opulence affords. Even worse than the Prioress is the worldly Monk, whose wealth makes a mockery of his vow of poverty and whose heretical theology makes a mockery of his orthodox pretensions. As if the Prioress and Monk were not cause enough for scandal, the Friar plumbs new depths of depravity, committing acts of fornication and adultery, getting maidens pregnant and begging from the rich so that he can keep up his life of lechery and luxury. The rollcall of reprobates continues: the shady Merchant, the pleasure-seeking Franklin, the avaricious Physician, the formidable and self-serving Wife of Bath, the utterly uncouth Miller, the dishonest Manciple, the corrupt and lecherous Summoner, and last and perhaps worst, the corrupt Pardoner, who makes a living selling fake relics to the gullible faithful.

In the midst of this iniquity, Chaucer kindles candles of sanctity to lighten our hearts and enlighten our way. There is the conscientious Clerk, a student who prefers poverty and a life of learning over the comforts of the world. There is, especially and magnificently, the poor Parson, who exemplifies the calling of a good and holy priest, putting his hypocritical neighbors to shame with his life of simple service to the farthest-flung members of his flock; and there is his brother, the Ploughman, who, living in peace and perfect charity, loving God above all, is the epitome of a truly holy layman. And so it is that Chaucer seasons his largely objectionable menagerie of miserable sinners with a couple of saints, one representing the clergy and the other the laity.

If the General Prologue should be essential reading for every Catholic, or at least those lines which depict the holiness of the Parson and the Ploughman, most people will not have the leisure or the liberty to read all of the tales that the pilgrims tell on their way to Canterbury. We will look at just one of the many that we might have selected, "The Nun's Priest's Tale", in the hope that it will serve to whet the reader's appetite for more.

"The Nun's Priest's Tale" is a fable about a rooster called Chauntecleer and his favorite hen, whose name is Pertelote. As with the more famous fables of Aesop, this fable has a definite moral message. Chauntecleer has a nightmare in which he has the vision of a villainous fox, its tail and both ears tipped with black to give it diabolically symbolic features. There then follows a discourse by Pertelote on dreams in which she dismisses them on essentially materialistic grounds as being meaningless, to which Chauntecleer responds with a lengthy riposte in which he cites biblical sources for the prophetic power to be gleaned from dream visions. The tale contains ironic references to the Fall of Adam, not least because the whole fable is essentially a retelling of the story of man's Fall. Chauntecleer can be seen to represent Adam, and his seven wives would appear to signify the seven deadly sins, with Pertelote, as the first and favorite of the seven, representing pride. In the midst of the rambunctious humor with which the tale is replete, there is a deeply theological meditation on the relationship between predestination and the freedom of the will. As the story unfolds, Chauntecleer, in the symbolic role of Adam, is tempted by a real-life diabolical fox who flatters the rooster, playing on his pride. Having trapped Chauntecleer in his jaws, the fox falls through the foolishness of his own pride, enabling Chauntecleer to escape and fly up into a tree, symbolic of the Cross of

Christ. We see, therefore, in this one tale the whimsical and wistful melding of *levitas* and *gravitas* that characterizes Chaucer's work.

Before we leave our discussion of *The Canterbury Tales*, we should consider Chaucer's English, which is called Middle English, to distinguish it from Old English, in which the *Beowulf* poet writes, and the modern English that comes after it. Whereas the Old English of *Beowulf* is very Germanic and very foreign to modern English speakers, the English of Chaucer is recognizable, at least with a modicum of effort. It is, however, more difficult to read than Shakespeare, who writes in Early Modern English, so many readers might find it very challenging. For this reason, an interlinear translation, which contains a modern translation side by side with the original text, will enable the reader to compare the Middle English original with the modern version.

Readers should also be warned that some of Chaucer's tales are somewhat bawdy, if not exactly raunchy, "The Miller's Tale" especially. Even though the overarching moral of these tales is profoundly Christian, some readers might be offended by the way in which some of them are told. As for Chaucer's ultimate purpose and motive for writing *The Canterbury Tales*, it is evident in the tale told by the saintly Parson, which is a lengthy treatise on the nature of the seven deadly sins and of the importance of repentance. It seems to have been the first of the tales to have been written and was positioned as the last to be told, signifying that the overarching theme of "The Parson's Tale" reflects the overarching theme of the work as a whole.

10

Sir Gawain and the Green Knight

The author of the late medieval Arthurian romance *Sir Gawain and the Green Knight* is unknown. He was a contemporary of Geoffrey Chaucer, which means that he was writing in the late fourteenth century, and he is probably the author of three other works, including the long allegorical poem *Pearl*.

Although the Gawain Poet was living and writing at the same time as Chaucer, they moved in radically different cultural worlds. Chaucer was based in London, which was then, as now, much more cosmopolitan than the rest of the country. Chaucer's language, which melded the Norman French of the aristocracy with the Anglo-Saxon Germanic tongue of the general population, would become the model of written English, which is why Chaucer is sometimes called the father of English poetry or the father of English literature. His literary style was influenced by the poetry of the embryonic European Renaissance, with its formal patterns of meter and rhyme.

The Gawain Poet, on the other hand, lived in the rustic hinterlands of the English west midlands, in the area that had been the kingdom of Mercia in Anglo-Saxon times. His poetry shows less European influence than Chaucer's, relying on older, indeed Old English verse forms, dating back to the time of *Beowulf* in the early eighth century, more than six hundred years earlier. In addition, the dialect in which the Gawain Poet wrote was closer to the Old English of Anglo-Saxon times than to the Middle English, with its French admixture, in which Chaucer wrote. For this reason, *Sir Gawain and the Green Knight* needs to be translated into modern English in order to be understood, whereas Chaucer's *Canterbury Tales* can be read and understood, with a little due diligence, by modern readers.

As for the poem itself, it tells the story of Sir Gawain, a noble knight of King Arthur's court, and his adventures in the quest to find the mysterious and magical Green Knight. The story begins in the Christmas season, when Sir Gawain accepts the Green Knight's challenge in an act of humble loyalty to the king, and resumes on the following All Souls' Day, when Sir Gawain sets out on his quest. This dating of the main events of the story in accordance with significant dates on the liturgical calendar conveys the poet's Christian allegorical intentions. The Feast of All Souls (November 2) is the date on the calendar in which the souls in purgatory are remembered. Sir Gawain's own quest, as we shall see, is purgatorial. It is the means by which his sinful soul is purged through the testing of his virtue.

Sir Gawain sets out with the right intentions and with holy will, telling King Arthur that he must keep his promise to seek the Green Knight "as God will my guide" (p. 36).[1] The allegorical symbolism continues with the poet's lengthy description of the significance of the pentangle that Sir Gawain wears as his coat of arms and which is

[1] *Sir Gawain and the Green Knight*, trans. J. R. R. Tolkien (New York: Ballantine Books, 1980). Text references are to page numbers.

emblazoned on his shield. We are told that the pentangle is known colloquially as the endless knot, signifying eternity, and that it symbolizes numerically the Five Wounds of Christ and "the Five Joys" that Christ had given "to Heaven's courteous Queen" (p. 39). In honor of the latter, Sir Gawain had an image of the Blessed Virgin on the inner side of his shield, which served as an emblematic plea for her protection in battle, "that when he cast his eyes thither his courage never failed" (ibid.). Finally, we are told that the pentangle also signifies five knightly virtues: free-giving, friendliness, chastity, chivalry, and piety. When Sir Gawain sets off on his quest, therefore, he is not merely well intentioned but is also well armed, both physically and spiritually.

Having begun the quest on the purgatorial Feast of All Souls, he continues right through the penitential season of Advent in pursuit of the elusive domain of the mysterious Green Knight. Then, on Christmas Eve, lost in a barren wilderness, he prays to the Blessed Virgin for help:

> The knight did at that tide
> his plaint to Mary plead,
> her rider's road to guide
> and to some lodging lead.
>
> (p. 41)

A little later, still on Christmas Eve, he prays again, to Christ and His Mother, that he might find some haven in which he can hear Mass and go to Matins on Christmas morning. He then prays the "Pater" (the Our Father), the "Ave" (Hail Mary), and the "Creed", and he invokes "the Cross of Christ" and makes the sign of the cross three times. At the end of the third signing of himself, he sees a moated mansion, an instant answer to prayer and a Christmas gift.

The porter at the mansion's gate invokes St. Peter, connecting the entrance to the mysterious mansion with St. Peter's Gate, which, in this poem as in Dante's, denotes the entrance to purgatory. During his stay in this strange place, he is tempted three times by the beautiful lady of the manor, who endeavors to seduce him while the lord of the manor is out hunting. Each time, he succeeds in keeping his vow of chastity. He does, however, succumb to the lady's offer of a gift of a green girdle, which she claims will protect him from death in any mortal combat. Since he is about to face the magically empowered Green Knight, fully expecting to be killed when he does so, he secretly accepts the gift.

When Sir Gawain finally meets the Green Knight, the latter reveals that he was the lord of the mysterious mansion and that it was he who had instructed his beautiful wife to test Sir Gawain's chastity:

> I sent her to test thee, and thou seem'st to me truly
> The fair knight most faultless that e'er foot set on earth!
>
> (p. 92)

The Green Knight then rebukes Sir Gawain for his act of deception in keeping secret from him the gift of the green girdle, a sin for which Sir Gawain receives a token wound. Mortified, Sir Gawain confesses his sin and curses the covetousness and cowardice that had caused him to accept the gift, begging the Green Knight's forgiveness. At this point, the Green Knight is revealed as a priest-figure, acting *in persona Christi*, as he absolves Sir Gawain of his sin in a doctrinally accurate depiction of the sacrament of penance:

Thou has confessed thee so clean and acknowledged
  thine errors,
and hast the penance plain to see from the point of
  my blade,
that I hold thee purged of that debt, made as pure
  and as clean
as hadst thou done no ill deed since the day thou
  wert born.

(p. 93)

Returning from his quest as a wiser, nobler man, Sir
Gawain vows to wear the green girdle as a remembrance of
his sin and as an aid to his continued quest for the humility
that is indispensable to sanctity. In some sense, therefore,
this particular Knight of the Round Table might be said to
have discovered the Holy Grail, metaphorically at least, or,
in any event, the keys to the kingdom of heaven.

11

Romeo and Juliet

There are two ways of reading *Romeo and Juliet*, one of which is correct, in the sense that it is the way that Shakespeare meant it to be read and understood, and the other is incorrect, in the sense that it violates and perverts Shakespeare's intentions.

The incorrect way of reading the play, which is the way that modern critics and teachers read it and teach it, involves what might be called a romantic reading. This way of seeing the play perceives the love between Romeo and Juliet as being blameless and beautiful, the tragedy being blamed on the feuding families and especially the parents. The correct way of reading the play is what might be called the moral or cautionary approach in which the tragedy is caused by the abandonment of reason in the face of erotic love or communal hatred.

Romeo sets the scene for his own iconoclastic approach to virtue at the very beginning of the play when he expresses scorn and contempt for Rosaline's vow of chastity, a prefiguring of the same contempt for chastity and virginity that he will show at the beginning of the famous balcony scene. He also describes love as "madness" (1.1.191),[1]

---

[1] William Shakespeare, *Romeo and Juliet*, ed. Joseph Pearce, Ignatius Critical Editions (San Francisco: Ignatius Press, 2011). Text references are to act, scene, and line.

demonstrating his enslavement to, and his enshrining of, mere emotion to the exclusion of the Christian under-standing of love as a rational choice to sacrifice oneself for others. As for Juliet, Shakespeare presents her as being considerably younger than she is in the source poem by Arthur Brooke that inspired the play. Surely it is no mere coincidence that Shakespeare makes Juliet only thirteen years old, the same age as his own daughter at the time he was writing the play. Romeo, on the other hand, is old enough to defeat the fearsome Tybalt with his swordsman-ship. He is, therefore, considerably older than Juliet, who is a mere child.

The imagery that Shakespeare employs with respect to the first kiss between the lovers is that of the exchange of sin, an imagery that reemerges with Juliet's kissing of Romeo's poisoned lips, prior to her stabbing herself fatally with his dagger, the latter act being itself an image of the deadly nature of their sexual union. As for the nature of Romeo's love for Juliet, it is as unhealthy as his earlier obsessive and ultimately lustful "love" for Rosaline, which is made clear in the Prologue to act 2 when we are told by the dispassionately objective voice of the Chorus that Romeo is "belov'd, and loves again, / Alike bewitched by the charm of looks" (lines 5–6). Nothing has changed. He "loves" in the same way. He is bewitched erotically by mere physical beauty. How indeed could his feelings for Juliet be otherwise when he had never seen her or spoken to her before and does not even know her name?

After Juliet's symbolic "fall" from the balcony, seduced by Romeo who stands symbolically among the fruit trees in the garden below, the two bewitched lovers descend into an idolatrous relationship in which each deifies the other, preferring their shared darkness to the light of either the sun or the moon. "If love be blind, / It best agrees with night"

(3.2.9–10), says Juliet. "Heaven is here / Where Juliet lives" (3.3.29–30), says Romeo in the following scene.

Throughout the play, the palpable absence of the cardinal virtues of prudence and temperance paves the way for disaster. The absence of such virtue in the lovers is exacerbated by its absence in other crucial characters who, being older, are perhaps even more culpable than the play's principal protagonists. As Friar Lawrence states, such "violent delights have violent ends" (2.6.9).

Although Friar Lawrence begins by giving sagacious advice, he fails to practice what he preaches in his rash agreement to marry the lovers in undue haste in the naive hope that the marriage might bring peace between the feuding families. He confesses his foolishness, accepting whatever punishment might be due to him, but is told by the Prince at the end of the play that "we still have known thee for a holy man" (5.3.269), a judgment that has been borne out, for the most part, by his actions. The same can hardly be said of the other characters. Capulet begins with a seeming desire to protect his child from a premature marriage but then insists upon forcing her into an unwanted marriage to Paris; the Nurse fails to support Juliet, even suggesting that her young charge proceed with the bigamous marriage. It is clear, therefore, that Juliet is betrayed by those who should have saved her from her own immature folly. This failure on the part of the adult characters serves as a moral counterpoint to the treacherous passions of youth. It is as though Shakespeare is illustrating that the young will go tragically astray if not restrained by the wisdom, virtue, and example of their elders. The final tragedy is that this lesson is learned by the Capulets and Montagues only in the wake of the deaths of their children. The lesson *is* learned, however, and the consequent restoration of peace provides a sad but consoling catharsis. Whether such a cathartic turn can be considered a happy ending is a moot point. It is, however, an ending that restores not only peace but sanity to the surviving protagonists, and this is surely a source of joy, even if a joy tinted with sorrow.

Ultimately, the peace that reigns at the end of *Romeo and Juliet* is much greater than the worldly and merely political peace that emerges in Verona. It is the knowledge imparted in the midst of the tragedy by Friar Lawrence that "a greater power than we can contradict / Hath thwarted our intents" (5.3.153–54). The greater power of divine providence is not contradicted. Its harmony and its peace remain. It cannot be thwarted by the imprudent impudence of the sinful intentions and actions of those who defy and deny the moral law.

"This sight of death is as a bell" (5.3.204), says Lady Capulet, indicating that death itself is the knell of doom that brings the feuding parties to their senses. "All are punish'd" (5.3.294), says the Prince, acknowledging the bitter price of the sinful disregard of virtue.

The Merchant of Venice

The Merchant of Venice is perhaps the greatest and indubitably the most controversial of Shakespeare's comedies. It has been misunderstood and misconstrued to such a degree, however, that it is often seen as a tragedy, not a comedy. Such is the critical blindness of the age in which we find ourselves.

Prior to a discussion of this critical blindness and the reasons for it, let's look at the play itself.

The Merchant of Venice is a tensely wrought and yet delightful comedy, centered on the necessity of self-sacrificial love. In terms of its form, it works in two distinct ways, which might be perceived visually as the horizontal forward movement of the plot and the vertical moral movement between the virtuous precepts of Belmont and the venal viciousness of Venice. With respect to the horizontal forward movement of the plot, it has three distinct focal "knots", each of which is a moral test: the test of the caskets, the test of the trial, and the test of the rings. In each case, the passing of the test signifies a movement heavenward from the City of Man (Venice) to the City of God (Belmont).

The purpose of the first of the tests is the winning of the hand of the heavenly Portia in marriage. Portia, heiress to the mysterious otherworldly realm of Belmont, cannot be won in marriage by those who value gold or silver but only by those who embrace the leaden casket, signifying death itself. To be worthy of the virtuous love of the virtuous Portia, one must be willing to die to oneself so that one can lay down one's life for the beloved.

The second of the tests is the test of the trial, or the testing of Shylock, in which Portia, in disguise as a lawyer, endeavors to persuade Shylock to abandon his demand for vengeance and to embrace instead the necessity of showing mercy that he might receive mercy. Her speech on "the quality of mercy" (4.1.184)[1] is one of the most beautiful monologues that Shakespeare ever wrote, the beauty and morality of which have all too often been eclipsed by the critical misreading of the play. But more on that presently.

The final test, the test of the rings, is set by Portia to test the fidelity of Bassanio, who had won her hand in marriage by his choice of the leaden casket. Is he true to his word? Will he really lay down his life for her in embracing the self-sacrificial bond of the sacrament of marriage, signified by the ring that Portia had given him? Portia, still in disguise as the lawyer, persuades him to part with the ring, illustrating his weakness and his unwillingness to be true to his bond. Portia, having exposed Bassanio's infidelity and weakness, does not condemn him but forgives him in an act of mercy, in stark contrast to the vengeful Shylock, who had resolutely refused to show mercy and forgiveness to Antonio in the trial scene. In this final test, therefore, Portia shows herself to be practicing what she had preached in the beautiful "quality of mercy" speech.

---

[1] William Shakespeare, *The Merchant of Venice*, ed. Joseph Pearce, Ignatius Critical Editions (San Francisco: Ignatius Press, 2009). Text references are to act, scene, and line.

Having surveyed the plot of *The Merchant of Venice* in its panoramic entirety and integrity, we can see how it has been woefully misread by those modern misreaders of the play who have turned the comedy of the three tests into the "tragedy of Shylock". Whereas the virtuous Portia is present and plays a crucial role in all three of the tests that form the focal points of the play, Shylock is present only in the second of them. Compared to Portia, Shylock is peripheral. Since this is clearly the case, we might wonder why he has stolen the show from the heavenly heroine. The reason lies in the alleged anti-Semitism of which he is perceived to be a victim.

In order to clear the play and its author of the charge of anti-Semitism, we need to see *The Merchant of Venice* through Shakespeare's eyes and through the eyes of his contemporary audience. The first thing to understand is that Shakespeare and his audience would have had very little contact with any real-life Jews because the Jews had been expelled from England during the reign of Edward I three hundred years earlier. On the other hand, the only moneylenders practicing usury in Elizabethan England were the Puritans, the practice of usury being condemned by the Church but condoned by John Calvin. Since it was illegal to present contemporary political and religious issues on the stage, it was not possible for Shakespeare to represent his villainous usurer as a Puritan. He does so surreptitiously, bypassing the censorship of the time, by presenting his usurious villain as being ostensibly Jewish. The allegorical mask would have been perceived by his audience as a thinly veiled euphemism for the Puritan moneylenders who were making themselves very unpopular in Elizabethan England. Since the Puritans were also opposed to the theatre and would eventually succeed in having all theatres in England closed down, Shylock would have been reviled by the audience—but not as a Jew.

The foregoing having been said, it should also be noted that the anti-Jewish sentiment in the play is not racist but economic and theological. First, a close reading illustrates that Shylock is loathed primarily for his practice of usury and not for the practice of his faith. Insofar as Judaism is mentioned, it is considered in religious, not racial, terms. The Jews are seen to be wrong in their refusal to accept the divinity of Christ, an honest theological perspective that does not constitute anti-Semitism. When Shylock's daughter, Jessica, elopes with Lorenzo and becomes a Christian, she is embraced and accepted. We are told that her "blood" has no more in common with Shylock's than red wine has with white (see 3.1.39–42), indicative of a nonracial perspective with respect to the differences between Christians and Jews.

In conclusion, let's compare the character of Shylock with two similarly miserly characters in the works of Charles Dickens, one of whom is Christian and the other Jewish. Ebenezer Scrooge is such a central figure in *A Christmas Carol* that we would not feel that the work had been violated unduly were it to be given the new title of *Scrooge*. On the other hand, the figure of Fagin in *Oliver Twist* is not a central character, though an important one, which would make a change of title to *The Tragedy of Fagin* an absurdity. Shylock has more in common with Fagin than Scrooge. He is not the central character in the play, nor is he present in anything but a peripheral sense in two of the three focal points of the plot. He needs to be put in his place so that we can see the comedy that Shakespeare wrote and not the travesty of the tragedy that the critics have erected in its place.

13

The Merry Wives of Windsor

The original title of the delightful comedy *The Merry Wives of Windsor* was *Sir John Falstaff and the Merry Wives of Windsor*. This is hugely significant because the play is largely a vehicle or an excuse for the lampooning of the character of Falstaff, who had made his first appearance in *Henry IV, Part 1*. In that play, Falstaff's character had originally been named Sir John Oldcastle, who had been one of the leaders of the Lollards, a proto-Protestant sect instituted by John Wyclif. Sir John Oldcastle led a failed rebellion in 1417 to overthrow the king and was subsequently hanged. He was later immortalized as a Protestant martyr in John Foxe's *Book of Martyrs*, published in 1563. It is, therefore, hardly surprising that Shakespeare's depiction of Oldcastle as a disreputable drunk and coward should outrage the Protestants of his time. Bowing to pressure, the character's name was changed to Sir John Falstaff, although Shakespeare has Prince Hal refer to him as "my old lad of the castle" (1.2.42),[1] keeping the provocative connection alive, albeit only allusively.

In *Henry IV, Part 2*, Prince Hal's conversion and rite of passage from dissolute youth to the fullness of responsible

---

[1] William Shakespeare, *Henry IV, Part 1* (New York: The Modern Library, 2011). Text references are to act, scene, and line.

kingship, following his accession to the throne as Henry V, is made manifest in his professed rejection of Falstaff and his degenerate lifestyle. "I know thee not old man", he tells him. "Fall to thy prayers" (5.5.47).

This brief character portrait of Sir John Falstaff serves as the background and the curtain-raiser to *The Merry Wives of Windsor*, which was written, so it is said, following Queen Elizabeth's desire for a comedy that would show "Falstaff in love".

Apart from Falstaff, whose incorrigible vanity serves as the humorous inspiration and dramatic driving force for the comedy, the principal characters are Master and Mistress Page and their friends, Master and Mistress Ford; Anne Page, the Pages' daughter, a virtuous maiden; and the three suitors to Mistress Paige: Slender, Dr. Caius, and Master Fenton.

Falstaff, blinded by his vanity, sends love letters to Mistress Page and Mistress Ford in the conceited belief that they are attracted to him. His primary motivation is not lustful but purely mercenary. He is short of the funds necessary to continue his drunken, debauched lifestyle and believes that these married ladies will keep him in the lap of luxury in return for his amorous favors. Upon receipt of the letters, the two "merry wives" decide to have fun at Falstaff's expense, feigning their love for him and their willingness to cuckold their husbands at his adulterous behest. Throughout the remainder of the play, Falstaff is made to look increasingly absurd and ridiculous, falling into folly after folly, outwitted by the wives and by his own self-conceited blindness.

A humorous subplot is provided by the jealousy of Master Ford, who is too ready to believe the worst of his wife, prefiguring in comic form the tragic and destructive jealousy of Othello.

Paralleling the "love" of Falstaff is the love of the three suitors for Mistress Page, two of whom are unworthy of her hand in marriage and whose advances are clearly unwanted. One of these two unworthy suitors, Master Slender, is in league with his cousin, Justice Shallow. Several scholars have shown convincingly that Justice Shallow and Master Slender are thinly veiled caricatures of Justice William Gardiner and his stepson, William Wayte, with whom Shakespeare had crossed swords in court in 1596, only a few months before his writing of *The Merry Wives of Windsor*, which was probably written early in 1597. Justice Gardiner was evidently a disreputable character "who defrauded his wife's family, his son-in-law, and his stepson, oppressed his neighbors and fleeced his tenants".[2] His stepson, William Wayte, was equally disreputable, being described as "a certain loose person of no reckoning or value, being wholly under the rule and commandment of the said Gardiner",[3] reflecting Slender's relationship to Justice Shallow in Shakespeare's play. In 1596, Wayte had petitioned the court, probably at Gardiner's behest, craving "sureties of the peace against William Shakespeare"[4] and others. Whereas Shakespeare's co-defendants in this court case included known Catholic recusants, Justice Gardiner was "one of the extreme Puritans"[5] who had boasted in a report in 1585 of a raid on a Catholic home in which "papist" books, pictures, and a crucifix were discovered and confiscated. Such a man was Shakespeare's enemy and, so it seems, Shakespeare had "staged" his revenge by parodying him as Justice Shallow in his comedy.

[2] H. Mutschmann and K. Wentersdorf, *Shakespeare and Catholicism* (New York: Sheed and Ward, 1952), 119.

[3] Ibid.

[4] Ibid.

[5] Ibid.

The third suitor to Mistress Page and the one who ultimately wins her hand in marriage is Master Fenton, a reformed prodigal whose conversion to a life of virtue parallels the conversion of Prince Hal in *Henry IV, Part 1* and also serves as a counterpoint and foil to Falstaff's viciousness. Whereas the virtuous suitor wins the hand of his beloved, the vicious suitor is left empty-handed and becomes the object of public ridicule. Master Fenton, the reformed and repentant sinner, is, therefore, the mirror of whom Sir John Falstaff ought to be.

14

Julius Caesar

More than most of Shakespeare's plays, *Julius Caesar* begs a good many questions. Who are the heroes? Where are the out-and-out villains, the Machiavels, who are so evident in many of Shakespeare's other plays? Where are the women? Is their relative absence significant? What does it say about politics and politicians? What does it say about the people? As a play that showcases the art of rhetoric, what does it say about rhetoric itself? If the play is to be considered a tragedy, where is there evidence of nobility or the tragic flaw that is nobility's undoing? What is the moral perspective?

Before we begin answering the multifarious questions that *Julius Caesar* poses, let's look at the historical context in which it was written.

It seems likely that Shakespeare wrote the play shortly after the so-called Bishops' Ban had forbidden the printing of new English history plays. Prior to the ban, which became law in June 1599 at the behest of the Archbishop of Canterbury and the Bishop of London, Shakespeare had written many plays depicting episodes from English history in a manner that satirized his own time. Plays such as *Henry IV* (parts 1 and 2), *Henry V*, and *Richard II* were seen to be thinly veiled attacks on Elizabeth's anti-Catholic regime. Such satires were no longer legal under the ban. Prompted to look further afield for the setting of his plays in order to circumvent the law, Shakespeare relocated his drama to the ancient world, *Julius Caesar* being the first of several plays set in classical times.

Having placed the play in its historical context, let's begin to answer the questions that *Julius Caesar* asks.

The play is unusual in the sense that there are no identifiable heroes. Whereas Dante places Caesar's enemies, Cassius and Brutus, in the lowest circle of hell, in the company of Judas, being devoured eternally by the insatiably ravenous Satan, Shakespeare is much more nuanced in his pointing of the finger of blame.

Caesar is blinded by his own arrogance, dismissing the soothsayer's warning that he should "beware the ides of March" (1.2.18, 23).[1] Such arrogance leads to ignorance, rendering Caesar blind and deaf to all good counsel, ignoring the pleading of his wife and the warnings of Artemidorus, and, in consequence, leading him directly into the conspirators' trap.

Cassius is identified as a puritan. "He loves no plays" (1.2.203), Caesar complains. "He hears no music" (1.2.204). In this casting of the play's least lovable character as a thinly veiled Calvinist, an enemy of the stage and an enemy of the Church, Shakespeare is employing a satirical caricature that recurs in other works. Shylock in *The Merchant of Venice* is another such example, as is Malvolio in *Twelfth Night*. Such depictions of Puritan characters, superficially disguised as Jewish moneylenders, Roman conspirators, or Renaissance courtiers, enable the plays to maintain the satirical applicability to contemporary England that the Bishops' Ban had

[1] William Shakespeare, *Julius Caesar*, ed. Joseph Pearce, Ignatius Critical Editions (San Francisco: Ignatius Press, 2011). Text references are to act, scene, and line.

sought to prevent. Compare, for instance, Caesar's description of the puritanical Cassius with Lorenzo's cautionary words in *The Merchant of Venice*: "The man that hath no music in himself, / Nor is not moved with concord of sweet sounds, / Is fit for treasons, stratagems, and spoils. / ... Let no such man be trusted" (5.1.83–85, 88).[2]

Although Cassius is clearly identifiable as a puritan, Brutus is himself tainted with the puritanical brush in his self-righteous stoicism and his disdain for the very notion of monarchy. His refusal to heed the counsel of his wife, which could have made him think twice about his involvement in the treacherous conspiracy, echoes Caesar's own refusal to take his wife's wise counsel.

In the wake of Caesar's murder, we are tempted to sympathize with Caesar's friend Mark Antony, especially after we've experienced his rhetorical brilliance, which succeeds in turning us against the conspirators, even as it turns the mob against the conspirators. We are, therefore, manipulated by the power of rhetoric to join the mob as they rampage riotously through the streets, claiming innocent victims in their pursuit of the guilty as is always the way that mobs pursue justice.

It is not long before we witness that both sides are animated by the cynicism of realpolitik, pursuing immoral means to purportedly good ends. Mark Antony is seen at the beginning of act 4 condemning his own family members to death and breaking the promises he had made to the mob by diverting to himself and his allies the bequests that Caesar had left to the people. He is also seen to betray Lepidus the moment his back is turned. When Octavius complains that Lepidus has proven himself as "a tried and

---

[2] William Shakespeare, *The Merchant of Venice*, ed. Joseph Pearce, Ignatius Critical Editions (San Francisco: Ignatius Press, 2009). Text references are to act, scene, and line.

valiant soldier" (4.1.28), Mark Antony responds coldly that so is his horse.

In the final analysis, the most striking feature of *Julius Caesar* is that none of its principal characters are particularly virtuous. This is not unique in the Shakespearean canon. We think perhaps of *Romeo and Juliet*, in which none of the characters show much virtue except for the flawed and far-from-perfect Friar. It is, however, unusual to see the absence of virtue to such a striking degree. It is as though Shakespeare, echoing the words of Mercutio in *Romeo and Juliet*, is calling down a plague on all their houses, in the sense that he is pouring scorn on Caesar's vanity, on Antony's bloodthirsty opportunism, on Cassius' ambition, on Brutus' brutal idealism. Yet, unlike Mercutio, he is not cursing from the perspective of a worldly cynicism but from that of a believing Christian at a time when believing Christians were being tortured and put to death by the vanity of monarchs, by bloodthirsty opportunists, by political ambition, and by brutal idealism.

There is, however, another level of meaning that is all too often overlooked completely. It is the sound of silence within the play; the scream in the vacuum of the play's vacuity. It is the unheard and unheeded voice of the virtuous. It is the voice of Caesar's wife Calpurnia, which, if heeded, would have saved Caesar's life; it is the voice of Brutus' wife Portia, which, if heeded, might have caused Brutus to think twice about his involvement with the conspirators. It is the voice of the Soothsayer and of the augurers. It is the voice of Artemidorus, a teacher of rhetoric, whose note to Caesar is devoid of all rhetorical devices and direct to the point of bluntness. The note is not read, the voice is not heard, and the consequences are fatal.

All that was missing in the play is the one thing necessary: the still, small voice of calm that the proud refuse to hear.

15

Hamlet

Shakespeare's *Hamlet* is arguably the greatest play ever written. It is, however, also one of the most misread and misunderstood. One could write a book, or perhaps a whole shelf full of books, on the way in which the play is misconstrued by critics, or the manner in which it is sacrificed to the latest literary fads. To give but one example of such *Hamlet* abuse, a recent production of the play in England casts Hamlet primarily as the abusive boyfriend of the hapless Ophelia.

In the face of this latest provocative and slanderous assault on the Bard's most sublime and elusive hero, let's put the man and the play in perspective.

Before we get to the troubled relationship between Hamlet and Ophelia, let's begin by insisting that we need to place the play within the context of the political cauldron in which it was written. Doing so enables us to engage with the tragedy on a level of profundity that is simply not possible if we insist on reading it from the perspective of our twenty-first-century ignorance and arrogance, judging it with the superciliousness of what C. S. Lewis would call our chronological snobbery.

We will not understand the man who is Hamlet unless we endeavor to empathize, nay sympathize, with the rage he feels upon discovering that his beloved father has been murdered in cold blood by Claudius, who is a loathsome and manipulative Machiavel that commits fratricide and regicide, presumably after having already committed adultery with his brother's wife, Hamlet's mother. Furthermore, on the subtextual level, we will not understand Hamlet's rage against spies, such as Polonius, Rosencrantz, Guildenstern, and yes, even Ophelia, unless we understand Shakespeare's own rage against Elizabeth's spy network and its role in the arrest of Catholic priests, such as St. Robert Southwell, and Catholic laity, such as St. Anne Line, whom Shakespeare almost certainly knew well. With respect to Southwell, Shakespeare pays allusive tribute to the Jesuit poet in the famous graveyard scene ("Alas, poor Yorick!" [5.1.179]),[1] which plays upon lines from Southwell's poem "Upon the Image of Death". It is this subtext which illumines the inner heart and allegorical depths of the play, exposing the "something rotten in the state of Denmark" (1.5.90) as "something rotten" in the state of England.

Nor will it do to demonize Hamlet with claims that he is guilt-ridden and suspicious in every scene, that he indulges in misanthropy, and that he continually mopes in self-indulgent acedia. He has every right to be suspicious, considering the network of espionage that surrounds him and threatens to enmesh him, and his righteous anger against his murderous uncle and his disdain for the treacherous spies, posing as friends, is not synonymous with misanthropy. Even if he does hate these particular men, he doesn't hate mankind and is quite clearly a loyal friend to the honest Horatio.

So what about his "abusive" relationship with Ophelia? Isn't this worthy of our contempt?

The accusation of abuse springs, of course, from Hamlet's tirade against his beloved in the famous "get thee to a

---

[1] William Shakespeare, *Hamlet*, ed. Joseph Pearce, Ignatius Critical Editions (San Francisco: Ignatius Press, 2008). Text references are to act, scene, and line.

nunnery" scene (3.1.121). Let us put ourselves in Hamlet's
shoes. He knows that his uncle, King Claudius, has murdered his father. He knows that Ophelia's father is King
Claudius' spymaster. He is understandably outraged when
he discovers that two of his trusted friends, Rosencrantz
and Guildenstern, are in the employment of this treacherous spy network. How do we think that Hamlet will
feel when he discovers that the woman he loves has also
betrayed him, especially if he is aware that his meeting
with her is a setup? His anger might be shocking, but it
simply will not do to reduce it to the rantings of a male
chauvinist abusing his girlfriend.

As for the old chestnut that Hamlet is a hopeless and
self-indulgent procrastinator, it would be much fairer to see
him as one who does not act rashly but with prudence and
temperance. He refuses to act upon impulse, seeking to discover whether the apparition is an "honest ghost" (1.5.138),
nor does he succumb to the temptation to suicide, solil-
oquizing himself into a God-fearing rejection of the sin
of self-slaughter. He does not act until he has come to an
acceptance and embrace of divine providence, quoting the
Gospel and declaring that "the readiness is all" (5.2.214–15).
In the end, he lays down his own life so that the "something
rotten" in Denmark can be purged. Well might we agree
with the noble Horatio, as he holds his dead friend in his
arms, that flights of angels are singing Hamlet to his rest.
Horatio's words are a translation, with only a minor alter-
ation, from the Latin of the *In paradisum*, the antiphon of
the burial service following the traditional Requiem Mass.
Thus, Shakespeare ends possibly his greatest play by offering
a Mass for the repose of the "noble heart" (5.2.351) of his
hero, giving his heroic prince the Catholic burial service
that was now illegal in the "rotten" state of England.

16

Twelfth Night

If Shylock in *The Merchant of Venice* is a thinly veiled Puritan (see chapter 14), so is Malvolio in *Twelfth Night*. Maria, in act 2 of *Twelfth Night*, describes Malvolio explicitly as "a kind of puritan" (2.3.139),[1] and the critic Leslie Hotson has argued that Malvolio was modeled on the Puritan William Knollys, First Earl of Banbury, who was an object of ridicule in Elizabeth's court for his besotted efforts to court a teenage girl, well under half his age, reflecting Malvolio's preposterous efforts to woo Olivia. In a popular ballad at the time at which Shakespeare was writing *Twelfth Night*, Knollys is derided as "Party Beard ... the clown", a reference to his multicolored beard, which was white at the roots, yellow in the middle, and black at the ends. In the play, Maria refers to the color of Malvolio's beard as something of which he is absurdly proud, and Malvolia is lampooned for his vainglorious and foolhardy efforts to woo a young lady in much the same way as Falstaff is lampooned in *The Merry Wives of Windsor* and in the way in which the ballad lampooned Knollys. It is likely, therefore, that Shakespeare's audience would have seen Malvolio as a satirical representation of William Knollys.

---

[1] William Shakespeare, *Twelfth Night* (New York: Simon and Schuster Paperbacks, 1993). Text references are to act, scene, and line.

There is, however, a dark side to the real-life Malvolio, which would have made him a perfect subject for Shakespeare's ridicule and scorn. As a member of the Puritan party in Elizabeth's court, Knollys would have been an enemy of England's beleaguered Catholics and a staunch critic of the theatre, connecting the one with the other.

The fact that the Puritans considered the theatre to be a dangerous disseminator of papist ideas can be gleaned from a sermon by the Puritan preacher William Crashaw, delivered at St. Paul's Cross in London in 1608: "The ungodly plays and interludes so rife in this nation: what are they but a bastard of Babylon [a euphemism for Rome in puritanical Biblespeak], a daughter of error and confusion; a hellish device—the devil's own recreation to mock at holy things—by him delivered to the heathen and by them to the Papists, and from them to us?"[2] Astonishingly, this attack on "papist plays" by the puritanical Crashaw is noteworthy as being one of the pithiest putdowns of Western civilization ever made. In one terse, bombastic sentence, the entire legacy of the West is dismissed as being a contagious disease, passed from the devil to the Greeks, and then to the Romans and the Catholics until finally, via Shakespeare and his fellow playwrights, it had contaminated modern England. Two years later, in February 1610, Crashaw was again equating Shakespeare and his ilk to the devil in a sermon he preached to the Lord Governor of Virginia. On this occasion he fulminated that the greatest threat to the newly founded colony was to be found in Catholicism and the evils of the theatre: "We confess this action hath three great enemies: but who be they? even the Devil, Papists, and Players."[3] Ironically, William

---

[2] H. Mutschmann and K. Wentersdorf, *Shakespeare and Catholicism* (New York: Sheed and Ward, 1952), 102.

[3] Ibid.

Crashaw's son, Richard, one of the greatest of the metaphysical poets, would become a Catholic and would die in lonely exile in Italy in 1649.

Another dark and malevolent aspect of the Puritans, which explains Shakespeare's dark and malevolent portrayal of Malvolio, is the manner in which they were directly responsible for the persecution of England's Catholics, including members of Shakespeare's own family. In July 1586, Sir Francis Knollys, father of Sir William, urged the banishment of all recusant Catholics and the exclusion from public office of all who married recusants. Shakespeare's father had been forced from public office for his recusancy in 1576 and was fined for his recusancy in 1592. Such malevolence on the part of England's Puritans must have animated Shakespeare's imagination as he depicted the malevolence of Malvolio, whose very name, it should be remembered, means "ill will", or "wicked will". It is for this reason that we make a major error in our reading of either *The Merchant of Venice* or *Twelfth Night* if we allow ourselves to sympathize with the plays' villains. This is made clear by the Shakespeare scholar Oscar James Campbell:

> Malvolio is given the usual Elizabethan treatment for an insane man: he is bound and cast into a dark prison. This has seemed so brutal to many actors that they have often presented him as the pathetic victim of cruel horseplay. That was certainly not Shakespeare's intention. When at the end of the play Malvolio frantically rushes offstage, shouting, "I'll be revenged of the whole pack of you," Shakespeare expected his audiences to follow him with the scornful laughter that he ... thought it was the business of comical satire to arouse.[4]

---

[4] Oscar James Campbell, ed., *The Reader's Encyclopedia of Shakespeare* (New York: MJF Books, 1966), 903.

It is, therefore, in the context of such comical satire that we need to see the play, at least if we have any desire to see it as Shakespeare and his audience saw it. We should see the malevolence of Malvolio and Shylock as we would see the malevolence of Hitler or Stalin. And this is not merely hyperbole. Shakespeare had seen the tyranny of the Puritans at work in his own life and in the lives of his family, and he feared what would happen if they ever came to power as the dominant force in the state. In this fear he was justified and vindicated by history. Within fifty years of Shakespeare's writing of *Twelfth Night*, the Puritans stormed to power, killing the king and closing the theatres, and even banning the celebration of Christmas. In a tragic example of life following art, Malvolio would finally get the revenge he had promised.

17

Othello

Othello is the first of what might be considered a trilogy of tragedies written by Shakespeare during a particularly dark period of English history. Taken together with *Macbeth* and *King Lear*, both of which were written shortly afterward, *Othello* exhibits the angst and anger felt by Catholics following the reintroduction of laws that not only made the practice of the Catholic faith illegal but also made being a priest or sheltering a priest punishable by death. These laws were reintroduced by the new king, James I, in violation of his promise to grant religious liberty and tolerance upon his accession to the throne. First performed on All Saints' Day (November 1), 1604, *Othello* was written in the second year of the reign of James and shortly after the new anti-Catholic laws were put into force.

As a Catholic himself, Shakespeare would have shared with his co-religionists an intense anger toward the king for his act of treachery and would have shared their deep sense of desolation and despondency at the renewal of the persecution, following as it did so soon after the initial exhilaration at the queen's death and the king's accession. There is, therefore, no coincidence in the connection between King James and the character of Iago, the Machiavellian monster at the dark and deadly heart of *Othello*. In the source from which he drew inspiration for the play,

Cinthio's *Hecatommithi*, Shakespeare changed the name of Alfiero, the Machiavellian character, to Iago, a Spanish variant of the name James, thereby deliberately connecting his ruthless and cynical villain with England's new king.

In the very first scene of the play, Iago reveals himself in starkly satanic terms with his declaration that "I AM THAT I AM" (1.1.66),[1] the antithesis of God's declaration of Himself in Scripture as "I AM THAT I AM."[2] A couple of scenes later, Iago responds scornfully to Roderigo, dismissing the very notion of virtue and the grace that is necessary for its practice: "Virtue? A fig! 'Tis in ourselves that we are thus and thus" (1.3.319). In this solitary line, Iago declares himself to be not only a non-Christian but an anti-Christian. He is *homo superbus* (prideful man) who believes that he has the power to be what he wants to be without the need for God. Having hatched the plot to bring about Othello's downfall, his deceitful words "pour [a] pestilence into [Othello's] ear" (2.3.345), enflaming the Moor's latent jealousy through the insinuation that Desdemona is in an adulterous relationship with Cassio, thereby poisoning the Moor's love for his hapless wife.

Iago's actions remind us of Claudius' pouring of poison into the ear of Hamlet's father, a murderous act that is itself a metaphor for the lies poured into the ears of those whom Claudius deceives for his own cynical ends. Every word that Iago utters within earshot of anyone else is a deliberate deception, making it perilous for anyone, the reader included, to believe anything that he says to others. His true motives are only revealed in soliloquies. It is when he is alone and unheard that he reveals that his own

---

[1] William Shakespeare, *Othello*, ed. Joseph Pearce, Ignatius Critical Editions (San Francisco: Ignatius Press, 2014). Text references are to act, scene, and line.
[2] Exod 3:14 (Geneva Bible, 1599).

motive for desiring Othello's downfall is the suspicion that Othello had cuckolded him. He is, therefore, guilty of the same prideful jealousy that he seeks to enflame in the Moor. They share the same fatal flaw.

If it's easy to see the darkness in the hearts of Iago and Othello, it is more difficult to see into the heart of the doomed damsel, Desdemona. Is she as pure and chaste as many critics seem to believe? Does she warrant comparison with the Blessed Virgin, as the critic Peter Milward suggests?[3] Is she as immaculate as the Virgin and as blameless as the Virgin's Son, a spotless victim of the sins of others? In order to answer these questions, we need to begin with the reasons for her initial attraction to Othello. It is not his courtesy that attracts her, still less his practice of Christian virtue; it is the tales he tells of his adventures on the high seas and in strange lands, many of which are clearly fabrications. In short, she appears to be attracted by the lies he tells, an unpromising foundation for the building of a relationship.

Spurning her own father, Desdemona hangs on to every boastful word, devouring Othello's vaunts "with a greedy ear" (1.3.149), and sets about taking the initiative in the all-too-brief courtship that follows. Her father is shocked by Othello's account and is reluctant to believe that his daughter would "confess that she was half the wooer" (1.3.175). Desdemona has gained the husband that she desires and sacrifices her father's feelings in her decision to elope with the Moor. She acts rashly and recklessly, blundering naively into an ultimately abusive marriage that will lead to her death. The fact is that she is not a good judge of character. When asked by Emilia if her husband was not

---

[3] Peter Milward, *Shakespeare's Meta-drama: Othello and King Lear* (Tokyo: Renaissance Institute, 2003), 30.

jealous, she replies with an innocence that is the cankered fruit of ignorance: "Who, he? I think the sun where he was born / Drew all such humors from him" (3.4.27–28). Her hopeless naiveté is accentuated by the immediate arrival of a heatedly jealous Othello. Such weakness on Desdemona's part plays right into the hands of the fiendish Iago.

Although Desdemona is indeed "guiltless" (4.1.47) of the sin of infidelity of which she stands accused, she is guilty of crass credulity in her believing the fantastic yarns that Othello spun about his past adventures and about the "magic" (3.4.69) handkerchief that he had given her, and she is credulous in the extreme in eloping with a man whom she hardly knows on the strength of his tales of derring-do. She is, therefore, partially culpable for the perilous predicament in which she finds herself. She is guiltless of the sin of adultery for which she is killed but is culpable for her betrayal of her father and the recklessness inherent in her elopement.

The play's blameless victim is not Desdemona but Brabantio, the loving father and "kind lord" (5.2.128) who died of a broken heart after his daughter's desertion of him. This being so, it is an error to place Desdemona in the illustrious company of Shakespeare's noble and saintly heroines. She does not belong with Cordelia, a truly blameless victim, or with the sagaciously irrepressible Portia. Instead, she should be placed alongside Shakespeare's tragic heroines who fall through a fatal flaw in their character or through the bad choices they make. She belongs with the impetuously passionate Juliet or with the hopelessly weak Ophelia. We can feel great sympathy for her, as we can feel great sympathy for Juliet or Ophelia, but we cannot exonerate her totally. She suffers the consequences of her own irresponsible actions, though it might be conceded, to employ the words of Lear, that she is more sinned against than sinning.

If the misreading of Desdemona's character represents a misreading of the play, so does the failure to understand Othello's description of himself as "one that lov'd not wisely, but too well" (5.2.347). These words, among the most famous in all of Shakespeare's works, have been allowed to define Othello's character. It is as though we have allowed our understanding of the tragic hero, and by extension the whole tragedy of which he is a part, to be governed by his own final words of self-justification.

For a Christian, and it is perilous to our understanding of the plays to forget that Shakespeare is a Christian, love is always the laying down of the life of the lover for the sake of the beloved. Love is always to die to oneself so that one can give oneself fully to the other. In this sense, Othello never loved Desdemona. On the contrary, in an infernal inversion of the true meaning of love, Othello lays down the life of his beloved for the sake of his own jealousy, sacrificing her on the altar of his own prideful anger. This is not love but its opposite. Rather than being "one that lov'd not wisely, but too well", he was one that loved not wisely nor well enough.

In this darkest of tragedies, Shakespeare censures the age in which he lives, "the time, the place, the torture" (5.2.372), with a tale of darkness, told and tolled with the doom-laden and crushing weight of the playwright's own heavy heart.

18

King Lear

King Lear interweaves the story of Lear and his daughters with the parallel story of Gloucester and his sons in such a way that we cannot truly speak of plot and subplot but only of co-plots woven together with majestic skill. Lear is betrayed by the deception of his self-serving daughters, Regan and Goneril; Gloucester by the deception of his illegitimate son, Edmund. Cordelia, the loyal and faithful daughter of Lear, suffers the hardships of exile because of her father's blind arrogance; Edgar, the loyal and legitimate son of Gloucester, suffers the hardships of exile through his father's blind ignorance. Lear and Gloucester lose everything in the worldly sense but, in the process, gain the wisdom they were lacking. The overarching moral theme resonates with the Christian paradox that one must lose one's life in order to gain it, or with the words of Christ that there is no greater love than to lay down one's life for one's friends (see John 15:13). Lear and Gloucester embody the truth of the former; Cordelia and Edgar (and Kent), the truth of the latter.

At the beginning of the play, King Lear promises political power to those of his daughters who "love us most" (1.1.53).[1] He demands absolute loyalty to the state, above

---

[1] William Shakespeare, *King Lear*, ed. Joseph Pearce, Ignatius Critical Editions (San Francisco: Ignatius Press, 2008). Text references are to act, scene, and line.

all else. Caesar demands all. There can be no room for other loves. Goneril and Regan outdo each other in sycophantic promises of absolute allegiance. Cordelia is a recusant, refusing to render unto Caesar that which is not rightfully his, choosing instead to "love, and be silent" (1.1.64). She cannot offer king (or state) any allegiance beyond that which her conscience dictates is appropriate morally. The parallels with the position of Catholics during the tyrannical reign of James I is obvious.

In addition to the play's allegorical applicability to the politics of Jacobean England, especially in relation to the plight of Catholic recusants in the face of a king who demanded absolute allegiance as his "divine right", *King Lear* also serves as a profound meditation on the nature and meaning of wisdom. Paradoxically, the contemplation of the meaning of wisdom is revealed through the voice of the play's two "fools". The Fool, representing the presence of worldly wisdom in the first half of the play, is replaced in the play's latter half by another "fool", the exiled and disguised Edgar in the guise of "Poor Tom" (3.4.131), who represents the "foolishness" of the Cross (1 Cor 1:18, KJV). At the pivotal point in the play, when Lear experiences the "madness" of his conversion from the worldly wisdom of the Fool to the Franciscan foolishness of Poor Tom, the Fool disappears without rhyme or reason, as if he's been exorcized. The deepest insights in *King Lear* come, therefore, from those who come to wisdom through suffering, not from those, like the Fool, who seek comfort in comfort itself.

"Nothing almost sees miracles but misery" (2.2.168–69), says Kent, his words serving to introduce the exiled Edgar, who enters in rags declaring that "Edgar I nothing am" (2.3.21). It is in his very "misery", being "nothing" in the eyes of the world, that he is fit to see miracles, or fit to be the means by which others may see them. When

Lear first sets eyes on Edgar, who is disguised as Poor Tom, a "madman" (3.4.44), Edgar is reciting a line from a ballad about the Franciscans: "Through the / sharp hawthorn blows the cold wind" (3.4.45–46).[2] The connection with the Franciscans is apposite considering that St. Francis was known as the *jongleur de Dieu*—God's juggler, or a "fool for Christ"—who famously stripped himself naked in public. Alluding to the Ten Commandments and candidly confessing his sin, Poor Tom repeats the refrain from the Franciscan ballad. It is at this very moment that Lear, pricked with the hawthorn of conscience more than the cold wind on the heath, emulates the example of St. Francis by tearing off his clothes and proclaiming, "Off, off, you lendings!" (3.4.111). This moment of "madness" signifies Lear's conversion from worldly pride to poverty-embracing humility. It is the madness of the sanity that desires sanctity, the love of the Cross that is nothing but foolishness to the world.

King Lear's conversion is paralleled by the conversion of Gloucester, who has been cruelly blinded by his enemies. His blindness enables Shakespeare to play with the axiomatic paradoxes at the heart of the play: the blind seer, the wise fool, and the sane madman. "I stumbled when I saw" (4.1.19), Gloucester proclaims, alluding to his "blindness" (when he still had his sight) in believing the treachery of Edmund and in condemning the innocent Edgar. He continues with the equally paradoxical complaint that it is "the times' plague, when madmen lead the blind" (4.1.46), a barbed observation that is as applicable to Jacobean England as it is to anything happening in the play itself. Seeing more clearly now that he is blind, he speaks disdainfully of the lust of the eyes of which he had

---

[2] From the ballad "The Friar of Orders Gray".

himself boasted in the play's opening scene, condemning the "lust-dieted man" (4.1.69) who "will not see / Because he does not feel" (4.1.70–71).

The play's final scene finds Lear reunited with Cordelia, the daughter whom he had wronged in the play's first scene. Finally reconciled with her, he is ready to suffer with her at the hands of their enemies. "Come, let's away to prison" (5.3.8), he says, telling her that, together, they can take upon themselves the mystery of things, "as if we were God's spies" (5.3.17). In this politically charged speech, Shakespeare turns for inspiration to the poetry of the Jesuit martyr St. Robert Southwell, as he had done in earlier plays, such as *Romeo and Juliet*, *The Merchant of Venice*, and *Hamlet*. The phrase "God's spies" would have been seen as a thinly veiled reference to the Jesuits, the connection becoming unmistakable when connected with Southwell's phrase "God's spice" in his poem "Decease Release". This poem, written in the first person with Mary Stuart, Queen of Scots, as the narrator, on the eve of her execution, refers to the executed queen as "pounded spice" and continues thus:

> God's spice I was and pounding was my due,
> In fading breath my incense savored best,
> Death was the mean my kernel to renew,
> By lopping shot I up to heavenly rest.

Like the martyred queen of whom he wrote, Robert Southwell was also destined to be "pounded spice" whose essence is more pleasing and valued for being crushed: "God's spice I was and pounding was my due." As a Jesuit in Elizabethan England, Southwell had been one of "God's spies" who, being caught, became "God's spice", ground to death that he might receive his martyr's reward in heaven. "Upon such sacrifices" (5.3.20), Shakespeare exclaims through the lips of Lear, "the gods themselves throw incense" (5.3.21).

As for final words of the play, enunciated by Edgar, the saintly "fool", it is a lament for the contemporary England in which Shakespeare and his fellow Catholics found themselves:

> The weight of this sad time we must obey,
> Speak what we feel, not what we ought to say.
> The oldest hath borne most: we that are young
> Shall never see so much, nor live so long.
>
> (5.3.325–28)

Yet hope remains. "All friends shall taste / The wages of their virtue" (5.3.304–5), Albany had said a few lines earlier, "and all foes / The cup of their deservings" (5.3.305–6). Edmund, Goneril, Regan, and Cornwall are dead. It is true that Cordelia and Lear are also dead, but there is an inkling in Lear's final vision that the lips of Cordelia, and those of Lear himself, are about to "taste the wages of their virtue". And, of course, there is sublime hope in the fact that the kingdom is left in the hands of Edgar, whose baptized Christian conscience had restored Lear to his sanity. It is the meekness of Edgar that inherits the earth, not the Machiavellian madness of Edmund or the more benign secularism of the Fool. As with the climax of all good comedies, even those masquerading as tragedies, all's well that ends well.

19

Macbeth

Apart from *The Comedy of Errors*, *Macbeth*, a tragedy of errors, is the shortest of Shakespeare's plays. At only 2,107 lines, it is barely half the length of *Hamlet*, with which it is often compared. The date of its composition is not certain, but several clues within the text suggest strongly that it was first performed in 1606, shortly after the notorious Gunpowder Plot in November of the previous year. The discussion of "equivocation" in the play would seem to be an allusion to the trial of the Jesuit Henry Garnet, who was executed in May 1606 for his alleged complicity in the plot. In the same month, Shakespeare's daughter Susanna was fined as a Catholic recusant. It is, therefore, against this gloom-laden and doom-driven backdrop of intensified persecution that Shakespeare wrote this darkest of plays.

Considering that the latest wave of anti-Catholic persecution had been ushered in by the new Scottish king, James I, it is significant that Shakespeare should choose to write a play about a wicked Scottish king at this very time. Furthermore, although Macbeth is a real historical figure, it is surely more than mere coincidence that Mac-Beth means "son of Beth", a barely concealed suggestion that James is continuing in the tyrannous tradition of his predecessor, Elizabeth I. Considering that Elizabeth had ordered the execution of James' mother, Mary Stuart, the connection was a stroke of satirical genius on Shake-speare's part. Another stroke of satirical brilliance is pro-vided by Shakespeare's contrasting of the wicked Scottish king, Macbeth, with his great English contemporary and counterpart, St. Edward the Confessor. In doing so, he was highlighting the difference between the Machiavellian anti-Catholicism of contemporary England and the virtu-ous Catholic kings of the "merrie" English past.

Having set the scene in which the playwright settles down to write, let's examine the gloomy fruits of his muse.

The *objective* presence of the supernatural is established from the outset with the entry of the three witches. These malevolent forces are not the figment of someone else's imagination, because there is nobody else present to wit-ness them. They are alone, and therefore they stand alone, utterly independent. We are in the real presence of evil, an evil that really exists whether we like it or not, and not an evil that is merely the product of our fetid fetishes or our fevered imaginations. In its formal structure, there-fore, *Macbeth* places us unequivocally in a supernatural cos-mos, rendering implausible all materialistic interpretations of the play's intrinsic meaning. In consequence, we can see that Macbeth is not merely serving himself in his self-serving ambition; he is serving the devil.

The presence of objectively verifiable supernatural power at the beginning of the play parallels the beginning of *Hamlet* and, in truth, the two plays complement each other, the one being the inversion of the other. Hamlet begins in despondency but, assisted by the benign presence of the honest Ghost who exposes the crimes of regicide, fratricide, and adultery, he grows in wisdom and forbear-ance until, quoting the Gospel, he is willing to lay down his life for his friends and countrymen, exorcising the "some-thing rotten" in Denmark. Macbeth begins in glory, being lauded and lionized for his valor in battle but, succumbing to the malevolent presence of deceptive satanic power, he loses all sense of goodness and truth, until, forsaking the Gospel and embracing suicidal nihilism, he is willing to lay down the lives of his friends and countrymen on the altar erected to his own ambition, so that only his own death can exorcize the "something rotten" in Scotland.

There are other parallels between the two plays. Lady Macbeth's desire to "pour [her] spirits" (1.5.23)[1] into her husband's ear, poisoning him with words that justify her own murderous lust for power, echoes Claudius' pouring of physical poison into the ear of Hamlet's father, his murderous modus operandi serving as a metaphor for the way that he and other characters pour the poison of deceptive words into the ears of others. Similarly, Macbeth's confession to himself that the diabolical plot that he has hatched with his wife merits that "our poison'd chalice" (1.7.11) be placed "to our own lips" (1.7.12) reminds us of the fate of Queen Gertrude and King Claudius in *Hamlet*.

As pride takes pride of place on the throne of Macbeth's soul, he finds himself increasingly trapped in the narrow and narrowing confines of his own head, the self-centered god of his own contracted and constricted cosmos. As he speaks to himself in secret, divorcing himself from others, his subjective perception supersedes objective reality. His decay is, therefore, as much a decay of philosophy as it is a decay of morality. The more he thinks of himself, the less he thinks of others, and the less he thinks of others, the less he thinks of the Other, which is the truth that transcends the self. He begins to lose his sense of reality. Sin smothers reason so that the normal function of a man's

---

[1] William Shakespeare, *Macbeth*, ed. Joseph Pearce, Ignatius Critical Editions (San Francisco: Ignatius Press, 2010). Text references are to act, scene, and line.

mind, which is to seek and find the truth, is "smother'd in surmise" (1.3.140) until "nothing is but what is not" (1.3.141). Thus, Macbeth's nihilism, which will come to bitter and futile fruition in the final act with his dismissal of life as "a tale / Told by an idiot, full of sound and fury, / Signifying nothing" (5.5.26–28), is seen to have its roots in the play's opening act with his turning away from *fides et ratio* toward infidelity and irrationality.

Macbeth is thus revealed as the anti-Hamlet. Whereas Hamlet begins in the Slough of Despond, temperamentally tempted to despair, he grows in virtue throughout the play until he reaches the ripeness of Christian conversion and the readiness to accept his own death as part of God's benign providence: "Not a whit, we defy augury: there is a special / providence in the fall of a sparrow" (5.2.211–12); the "readiness is all" (5.2.215).[2]

Whereas Hamlet ends by defying "augury", Macbeth ends by defying everything except "augury". Hamlet grows in faith *because* he grows in reason; Macbeth loses his faith *because* he loses his reason.

Like Aristotle and St. Thomas Aquinas, Hamlet never loses sight of the distinction between the *essence* of things and their *accidental* qualities. He concerns himself with *definitions*, with the meaning of things, and with the distinction between those things that essentially *are* and those that only *seem* to be. "*Seems*, madam!", says Hamlet to his mother. "Nay, it *is*; I know not seems" (1.2.76; italics added). Hamlet does not make Macbeth's fatal mistake of allowing himself to become "smotherd in surmise" (1.3.140), nor does he succumb to Macbeth's irrational despair of believing that life signifies nothing. Hamlet knows that

[2] William Shakespeare, *Hamlet*, ed. Joseph Pearce, Ignatius Critical Editions (San Francisco: Ignatius Press, 2008). Text references are to act, scene, and line.

life is about what things *mean*, not what they *seem*, and
that the secret of life is learning to discover the difference
between the two. Whereas Hamlet knows that life is the
quest for the definite amid the clouds of unknowing, Macbeth loses his head and soul in the unknowing clouds of
his own sin-deceived ego. Far from seeing life as a quest,
Macbeth is left with nothing but his own bitter inquest
on life, "signifying nothing" (5.5.28). This is the "deepest
consequence" (1.3.126) of Macbeth's rejection of faith and
reason. In losing sight of the significance of others, or the
Other, he loses sight of the significance of everything else.
In choosing himself above others, he is not even left with
himself. He loses everything, even his own soul. He is left
with the "nothing" that is nothing else but the real absence
of the good that he has rejected.

20

Antony and Cleopatra

Following hot on the heels of *Macbeth* and being first performed in late 1606 or early 1607, *Antony and Cleopatra* might
be coupled with *Romeo and Juliet*, Shakespeare's earlier tragedy about erotic recklessness, written eleven years earlier.
If, however, Romeo and Juliet might be forgiven for the
follies of their head-weak and heart-strong youth, no such
excuse or mitigating circumstance applies to the characters
of Antony and Cleopatra. They are older and much more
seasoned in life and experienced in love. They should know
better. Their tragic weakness, the cause of their downfall, is
that they are grown-ups who refuse to grow up. Unable or
at least unwilling to accept their responsibilities, they wreck
their own lives and the lives of others on the recklessness
of their destructively self-indulgent passion.

The allegorical scene is set by the play's very first lines
that are spoken, significantly, by a character named Philo,
the Greek word for "love". Philo, the voice of authentic
self-sacrificial love, laments that Antony has forsaken such
love for its erotic antithesis, which pursues sexual self-
gratification. In the very first line, Philo expresses exas-
peration at Antony's "dotage" (1.1.2),[1] which "o'erflows

---

[1] William Shakespeare, *Antony and Cleopatra* (New York: Simon and Schuster Paperbacks, 2010). Text references are to act, scene, and line.

the measure" (1.1.2): "His captain's heart ... reneges all temper and is become the bellows and the fan to cool a gypsy's lust" (1.1.6–10). These lines are the cue for the entry of Antony and Cleopatra, whom we see for the first time, presumably exhibiting the intemperate "dotage" of their intoxicating lust for each other. Philo invites us to share in his own censorious disapproval of their behavior:

> Look where they come,
> Take but good note, and you shall see in him
> The triple pillar of the world transformed
> Into a strumpet's fool. Behold and see.
>
> (1.1.11–14)

The moral perspective being established by the voice of Love himself, the remainder of the play is the playing out of the inexorable consequence of the choosing of self-indulgent lust over self-sacrificial love. There are moments when Antony recognizes his slavery to sin and the consequences of his recklessness. "These strong Egyptian fetters I must break," he says, "or lose myself in dotage" (1.2.128–29). Apart from the self-destructive consequences of his erotic addiction, there are the wider political ramifications of his "dotage":

> I must from this enchanting queen break off.
> Ten thousand harms more than the ills I know
> My idleness doth hatch.
>
> (1.2.143–45)

As is so often the case, Shakespeare takes the drama to deeper allegorical depths through the intertextual employment of biblical allusions. It is, for instance, significant that Antony should send Cleopatra a pearl of great price. She is his heaven. His goddess. The object of his idolatry. As a token of his worship of her, he will sell everything he has: his wife, his country, the lives of his men. He offers the queen of his adulterous heaven everything he has. Every other person is betrayed; all duty is abandoned; every virtue is sacrificed on the altar erected to their vice.

If allusions to Scripture enable Shakespeare to plumb theological depths, nuggets of pure reason enable him to delve deep into axiomatic philosophical truths. We are told that Antony is culpable for the destructive consequences of his actions because he "would make his will lord of his reason" (3.13.4–5). When we try to subject reason to our will, rather than subjecting our will to reason, we are inevitably and inexorably on the path of self-destruction. We see this truth expressed and played out in many of Shakespeare's plays, a truth that exposes the evil consequences of the philosophy of Machiavelli in Shakespeare's own day and which prophesies the wicked consequences of the philosophy of Nietzsche, with its advocacy of the supremacy of pride over humility, and its call for the will to be made the lord of reason. It is for philosophical insights such as these that Shakespeare remains perennially relevant, a poet and prophet who, as Ben Jonson reminds us, "was not of an age but for all time".[2]

As the play plummets toward the inevitable downfall of its eponymous protagonists, we are not surprised to see the emergence of another allegorically charged character, who is aptly named Eros, a servant of Antony who is almost a mere personified abstraction, signifying erotic "love", or lust. Fulminating over Cleopatra's betrayal of him, Antony calls for his servant: "What Eros, Eros!" (4.12.33). It is, however, not the servant who enters on Antony's cue but

---

[2] From his poem, "To the Memory of my Beloved, the Author, Mr. William Shakespeare: and what he hath left us".

Cleopatra, connecting the queen with eros itself. She exits again quickly, fleeing from Antony's rage, and Antony once again calls for his servant: "Eros, ho!" (4.12.47).

Telling Eros of Cleopatra's treachery, Antony resolves to make a suicide pact with eros itself: "Nay, weep not, gentle Eros. There is left us ourselves to end ourselves" (4.14.25–26). He asks Eros to "unarm" him and Eros begins to remove his armor, which is allegorically suggestive of the way that erotic desire had disarmed Antony of every virtue. Keeping the suicide pact in mind, he tells Eros that they will walk "hand in hand" (4.14.61) in the afterlife in the realm of erotic love ruled over by "Dido and her Aeneas" (4.14.63), the erotically besotted lovers in Virgil's *Aeneid*, whom Virgil describes as being "prisoners of lust" who are "unmindful of the realm" (4.265),[3] neglecting their duties to their respective peoples. Well might Shakespeare make the intertextual connection between his own "prisoners of lust" and those of his illustrious predecessor!

Eros stabs himself, dying to "escape the sorrow of Antony's death" (4.14.13–14). Antony follows suit, declaring that he had learned the art of self-destruction from Eros:

> Come then, and, Eros,
> Thy master dies thy scholar. To do thus
> I learned of thee.
>
> (4.14.121–23)

He then stabs himself. The moral is plain enough. Those who will not be masters of erotic desire will be mastered by it, with self-destructive consequences. The scene ends with the body of the dead Eros and the mortally wounded Antony being carried offstage.

---

[3] Virgil, *The Aeneid*, trans. Robert Fitzgerald (New York: Vintage Classics, 1990). Text references are to book and line.

Cleopatra's words to Antony, in the final moments before his death, are characteristically self-centered:

> Hast thou no care of me? Shall I abide
> In this dull world, which in thy absence is
> No better than a sty?
>
> (4.15.70–72)

All that remains is Cleopatra's own selfish act of self-destruction, carried out in spite of Caesar's warning that he would kill her own children should she commit suicide. Her act of self-slaughter is, therefore, also a slaughter of the innocents. She chooses a serpent as the means by which she will take her own life, connecting the play's final scene to the Book of Genesis. She chooses the serpent as the weapon of self-slaughter because its venom "kills and pains not" (5.2.298). Cleopatra chooses her own comfort in death as she had chosen it in life. She is the antithesis of the Christian who is called to accept and embrace suffering by taking up his cross and following Christ. "Peace, peace!" (5.2.367), she proclaims as she holds the serpent to her chest. "Dost thou not see my baby at my breast that sucks the nurse asleep?" (5.2.368–69).

Lest we should fail to connect the fall of Cleopatra with the fall of Eve, Shakespeare has the Guard report that the serpent had left a trail of slime on "these fig leaves" (5.2.421), indicating clear proof of the means by which she had died. In making this final biblical allusion, we are invited to see Cleopatra as more than merely a tragic heroine from ancient history but as a representative of fallen Eve and, by extension, our representative also. She is an Everyman figure. She is who we are and who we are doomed to be if we will not accept the redemption offered by Christ.

21

The Tempest

One of the many mysteries surrounding the life of William Shakespeare is the reason for his early retirement, when he was still in his forties, at the height of his powers and still apparently in good health.

Shakespeare announced his retirement in dramatic fashion at the end of his final play, *The Tempest*, when Prospero walks on stage alone, after the final curtain has fallen, to announce that he has relinquished his powers. The fact that a character addresses the audience directly, breaking the spell that had sustained the viewers' suspension of disbelief, is seen by most critics as the playwright gatecrashing the conclusion of his own play to take his final bow.

Shakespeare's premature retirement was probably connected to the vituperative attacks on the theatre in general, and on Shakespeare in particular, by the increasingly powerful Puritans who considered both plays and players to be "heathen" and "papist". The Puritan preacher, William Crashaw, in a sermon preached in London in 1608, fulminated against "ungodly plays" that were "a hellish device—the devil's own recreation to mock at holy things—by him delivered to the heathen and by them to the Papists, and from them to us."[1] Two years later, in February 1610,

---

[1] H. Mutschmann and K. Wentersdorf, *Shakespeare and Catholicism* (New York: Sheed and Ward, 1952), 102.

Crashaw described "the Devil, Papists, and Players" as the "three great enemies".[2] Later the same year, a Royal Proclamation called for the due execution of all former laws against recusants, ushering in a new wave of persecution against Catholics. In the following year, the Puritan writer John Speed connected Shakespeare with the Jesuit Robert Parsons, describing them as "this Papist and his poet".[3] This, then, was the threatening and volatile backdrop to Shakespeare's writing of *The Tempest* in late 1610 or 1611.

As for the play itself, it has suffered the slings and arrows of outrageous abuse by modern critics. In many productions and readings of *The Tempest*, Caliban is lionized as a victim in spite of his boast that he would rape Miranda repeatedly if he had the opportunity to do so. His desire to force himself upon the virgin daughter of Prospero is glossed over so that Caliban can be seen as the victim and Prospero the villain. Perhaps, as the daughter of the villain, Miranda would presumably have gotten what she deserved had the "persecuted" Caliban had his way with her.

Such a perverse reading of the play is a consequence of the current manic race obsession, which has rendered large sections of the population as mad as the Nazis. To critical race theorists, race is much more important than rape, and the racist much worse than the rapist. Indeed, if the rapist is seen as the victim of the racist, it is crucial to empower the rapist at the expense of his victim. This, at any rate, is the fate that has befallen poor Prospero and his hapless and innocent daughter.

Let's look at how the critical race theorists misinterpret the play, then we'll look at the play Shakespeare actually

[2] Ibid.
[3] Ian Wilson, *Shakespeare: The Evidence* (New York: St. Martin's Griffin, 1999), 228.

wrote and the intention he clearly had with respect to its meaning.

In our race-obsessed age, Prospero is caricatured and stereotyped as a white imperialist and Caliban as a native-born islander, whom Prospero subjugates and treats as a slave. This racist stereotyping is then permitted completely to eclipse the whole plot and purpose of the play.

Let's look at the play itself as distinct from the ideological distortions of it.

Prospero is not an "imperialist" oppressor but has been shipwrecked on the island with his very young daughter, having been left for dead on the open sea by his political enemies. He is, therefore, an exile and a refugee. Caliban was born on the island, his mother being the witch Sycorax, who arrived on the island when pregnant with Caliban, whose father was apparently Setebos, a demon. He is, therefore, not a nonwhite human being but a monstrous being of some sort or another. Nor is he an aboriginal islander. There are none. It was a truly desert island until the arrival of the witch with Caliban in utero. Nor did Prospero treat Caliban badly. On the contrary, as he reminds Caliban, he had treated him

> with humane care, and lodged thee
> In mine own cell till thou didst seek to violate
> The honor of my child.
>
> $(1.2.346-48)^4$

Caliban does not deny the charge of attempted rape but boastfully claims that he would have violated the child repeatedly had he not been forcibly stopped from doing so:

---

[4] William Shakespeare, *The Tempest* (New York: Signet Classic, 1998). Text references are to act, scene, and line.

> O ho, O ho! Would't had been done!
> Thou didst prevent me; I had peopled else
> This isle with Calibans.
>
> (1.2.349–51)

It is at this moment that Miranda exclaims that Caliban is an "abhorrèd slave" (1.2.351), which no doubt condemns her in the eyes of the neo-puritan race-obsessives as a racist who should therefore have no complaints when the "slave" rapes her in vengeance. It is a mark of the illiteracy of these postmodern puritans that they fail to see that the word "slave" refers to Caliban's slavery to his lower nature, his inability to govern himself with virtue, his slavery to sin. It has nothing to do with chattel slavery. As for Prospero's treatment of Caliban following the attempted rape, what else was he meant to do? Might he not even have been justified in killing the would-be rapist of his daughter as the only safe way of protecting her? Caliban, if anything, should be grateful that his life has been spared. Instead, he forms an unholy alliance with a couple of low-life drunks in a plot to kill Prospero, luring them into his murderous scheme with the promise that they would be free to rape Miranda once Prospero is dead. It really does beggar belief that Caliban is seen as the victim and not the villain. The slavery to lust of Caliban and the two miscreants with whom he makes the unholy alliance is contrasted with the chastity of the young lovers, Miranda and Ferdinand, whose purity is symbolized by the game of chess that they choose to play when they find themselves alone together.

Over and above these aspects of the story, the play's overarching theme is the restoration of justice and the reconciliation of adversaries, which is brought about by the use of Prospero's powers, and those of his servant Ariel, which, combined, are meant to be understood allegorically as the power of the playwright to bring order out of chaos and concord from discord. This is the reason that Prospero's arrival on stage, after the fall of the final curtain, is so powerful. In his heartfelt farewell and his request for prayers, he is transformed, as if by magic, into Shakespeare himself:

> And my ending is despair,
> Unless I be reliev'd by prayer,
> Which pierces so, that it assaults
> Mercy itself, and frees all faults.
>> As you from crimes would pardon'd be,
>> Let your indulgence set me free.
>>> (act 5, epilogue)

22

Don Quixote

At the conclusion of his marvelous poem "Lepanto", G. K. Chesterton imagined the great Spanish writer Miguel de Cervantes setting his sword back in his sheath and smiling contentedly after he has played his part in the historic victory of the Christian fleet over its Turkish foe at the Battle of Lepanto in 1571. Chesterton concluded his poem with these lines as a way of showing that the victory was crucial to the survival of Christendom and its cultural fruits, epitomized and symbolized by Cervantes' classic novel *Don Quixote*, about "a lean and foolish knight [who] forever rides in vain" (line 141).[1]

Miguel de Cervantes fought heroically at Lepanto, receiving a serious wound to his left hand that he would wear as a badge of honor for the remainder of his life, as well he might. Born in Spain in 1547, he would not attain success as a writer until the publication of the first part of *Don Quixote* in 1605, when he was fifty-eight years old. The second part would appear ten years later, a year before his death. Cervantes was, therefore, a late bloomer and what might be called a one-hit wonder, his other works being largely unsuccessful during his own lifetime and largely forgotten today.

---

[1] G. K. Chesterton, "Lepanto", in *The Collected Poems of G. K. Chesterton* (New York: Dodd, Mead, 1949).

If, however, Cervantes can claim only one literary classic to his name, as distinct from the dozens of classics written by his great contemporary Shakespeare, he can claim to have written the most successful work of literature in the history of the world, at least in terms of global sales. It is generally accepted that *Don Quixote* is the all-time best-seller, outselling its nearest rivals, *A Tale of Two Cities* by Charles Dickens and *The Lord of the Rings* by J. R. R. Tolkien. As for its literary merit, we can trust the view of Maurice Baring, a fine writer who was himself the finest of critics, that "no book has such a good beginning as *Don Quixote*, and no book has a finer end".[2]

So what makes *Don Quixote* so special?

First, if not necessarily foremost, it was a first of its kind, arguably the first novel ever written, the progenitor of a whole new literary form. It is full of exciting action and is driven by the unlikely friendship of Don Quixote and his servant and traveling companion, Sancho Panza, the latter's almost cynical no-nonsense realism serving as an intellectual foil to Quixote's manically romantic fantasizing. At the novel's heart is the evident desire of Cervantes to satirize and lampoon the popular books of chivalry, the *libros de caballerías*, which were the pulp fiction of the day. This has been seen by some as evidence of a deep-seated cynicism, or at least an anti-romanticism, on Cervantes' part. Lord Byron, for instance, in his poem *Don Juan* argued that *Don Quixote* is an iconoclastic attack on civilization itself. Strong words indeed. The great Russian novelist Fyodor Dostoyevsky, on the other hand, regarded Don Quixote as the "most perfect ... of all the beautiful individuals in Christian literature", adding that "he is beautiful only

---

[2] Maurice Baring, *Have You Anything to Declare?* (London: William Heinemann Ltd., 1936), 195.

because he is ridiculous."[3] He then gets to the mystical and mysterious heart of the novel: "Wherever compassion toward ridiculed and ingenious beauty is presented, the reader's sympathy is aroused. The mystery of humor lies in this excitation of compassion."[4]

Dostoyevsky wrote these words as he was beginning to create the quixotic character of Prince Myshkin, the protagonist of his novel *The Idiot*, who was clearly inspired by Don Quixote and indeed modeled on him. Prince Myshkin's transparent goodness as well as his lack of guile and noble simplicity make him an object of ridicule in the eyes of the cynically worldly and yet evoke sympathy in those who admire his virtue and see something akin to wisdom in his innocence. It is for this reason that Sancho Panza, for all his own skepticism and jaded worldliness, is attracted to the "holy foolishness" of his master.

It is, therefore, in this light, perhaps, that we should read *Don Quixote*, seeing its protagonist as a holy fool with whom we should sympathize, even when he is at his most ridiculous. And yet there is a real danger in taking this quixotic foolishness too far. If we are not careful, we begin to see the foolishness as something that is an end in itself, as a divine madness separating faith from reason. This is a perilous path to take, leading to the heresy of fideism. *Don Quixote* can lead us in this direction, seducing us to sympathize with irrational faith over rational disbelief, or it can lead us in the opposite direction, enticing us to see all faith as madness. It is clear, however, that Cervantes intends to lead us in neither direction, both of which are inimical to the Catholic insistence on the intrinsic and indissoluble

---

[3] Fyodor Dostoyevsky, *Complete Letters*, vol. 3, 1868–1871 (New York: Ardis Publishers, 1988), 15.

[4] Ibid.

bond of faith and reason (*fides et ratio*). He leads us, in fact, to Don Quixote's conversion to the fullness of Catholic realism, philosophically understood, in which goodness is not married to madness, but in which sanctity and sanity are one and indivisible in the holy matrimony of *fides* with *ratio*. In short and in sum, Don Quixote is healed of his delusions at the end of the novel, regaining his sanity, which finds full and final expression in his reconciliation with Holy Mother Church.

"Blessed be the Almighty for this great benefit He has granted me!" he cries in a loud voice upon awakening from sleep during his final illness. "Infinite are His mercies, and undiminished even by the sins of men."[5]

"What mercies and what sins of men are you talking about?"[6] asks his niece.

"Mercies", Don Quixote answers, "that God has just this moment granted to me in spite of all my sins. My judgment is now clear and unfettered, and that dark cloud of ignorance has disappeared, which the continual reading of those detestable books of knight-errantry had cast over my understanding.... I find, dear niece, that my end approaches, but I would have it remembered that though in my life I was reputed a madman, yet in my death this opinion was not confirmed."[7]

Coming to his senses, he asks for a priest to hear his confession. The priest, after absolving him of his sins, announces that there is no doubt that he is at the point of death, "and there is also no doubt that he is in his entire right mind."[8]

[5] Miguel de Cervantes, *Don Quixote*, trans. Walter Starkie (New York: Signet Classic, 2001), 1045.
[6] Ibid.
[7] Ibid.
[8] Ibid., 1046.

"I was mad," Don Quixote says a little later, "but I am now in my senses."[9]

In sound mind and in a state of grace, "after he had received all the sacraments",[10] Don Quixote breathes his last.

And so this most enigmatic of novels concludes with the happiest of endings in which the madness of life is healed by the holiest of deaths. Let the final words belong to the words inscribed on Quixote's tomb:

> Here lies the noble fearless knight,
> Whose valor rose to such a height;
> When Death at last did strike him down,
> His was the victory and renown.
> He reck'd the world of little prize,
> And was a bugbear in men's eyes;
> But had the fortune in his age
> To live a fool and die a sage.[11]

On St. George's Day 1616, Miguel de Cervantes also breathed his last, as did William Shakespeare. It was singularly and surely providentially appropriate that the brightest jewels in the golden ages of Spanish and English literature should have taken their respective last bows together. It was also singularly appropriate that these slayers of dragons should have died on the Feast of St. George, true knights as they were, who had wielded their pens like lances in the service of the good, the true, and the beautiful.

[9] Ibid., 1047.
[10] Ibid., 1049.
[11] Ibid.

23

Paradise Lost

Although almost all the great writers prior to the mid-seventeenth century had been Catholic in either sympathy or practice, John Milton (1608–1674) took up the Protestant cause with revolutionary zeal. Following the victory of Cromwell's Puritan army in the English Civil War, he supported and defended the execution of King Charles I. Then, in 1660, when he was in the middle of writing *Paradise Lost*, he had strongly opposed the Restoration of the monarchy, which had signaled the ultimate demise of the Puritan "Commonwealth" that Cromwell had established and to which Milton had pinned his political and theological hopes.

Milton became so heterodox, denying the Trinity and therefore the true divinity of Christ, that it is arguable that he cannot justifiably be called a Protestant or even a Christian of any sort in C. S. Lewis' "merely Christian" sense of the word. And yet *Paradise Lost* is indubitably one of the true masterpieces of world literature, following in the noble epic tradition of Homer and Virgil and, in consequence, demands inclusion in any book focusing on the great works of literature. Nonetheless, and irrespective of positive readings of its indubitable literary merit by estimable critics, such as C. S. Lewis, Catholic readers of Milton's epic need to be aware of the heterodoxy that animates it.

This heterodoxy will be our focus, therefore, even though such a critique should not blind us to the glorious sweep of Milton's use of the English language, or his gifts as a storyteller, or his wonderful depiction of marital love in the prelapsarian Garden.

At the dark heart of *Paradise Lost* is the looming and alluring presence of Milton's Satan, whose powerfully portrayed characterization has elicited sympathy from many readers of the poem, from Percy Shelley's eulogizing of him in the early nineteenth century to modern manifestations of sympathy for him in our own time. With respect to the latter, an article in *The Atlantic*, in March 2017, discussed the fascination that Americans feel for the character of Lucifer in Milton's epic and how it manifests itself in the characterization of thoroughly modern anti-heroes on contemporary television, especially in *The Sopranos*, *Mad Men*, and *Breaking Bad*, all of which are seen to reflect in some manner the dark side of the American dream. This morbid fascination with Milton's archetypal anti-hero prompts Simon to ask a provocative question: What's so "American" about John Milton's Lucifer?

There is, however, another provocative question that must be asked if we are to avoid misunderstanding and misconstruing Milton's Satan. Regardless of how "American" he is, we need to ask how "Christian" he is.

At the heart of such a question is a paradox. From an orthodox Christian perspective, the real Satan is, at one and the same time, a Christian and an anti-Christian. He is a Christian in the sense that he knows that Christ is the Incarnate Son of God; he is an anti-Christian because he hates the Son as he hates the Father. He knows the Trinitarian God, and he hates him. He is not an unbeliever. He is a rebel who is at war with the reality in which he has no choice but to believe.

The demons in the Gospel do not deny the authority of Christ. They defy him, as far as they are able, and despise him, but they do not and cannot deny him. We see the same paradox in the manner in which Dracula, in the old movies, recoils in horror from the sight of a crucifix. He hates the symbol of the power of Christ, but he cannot help but retreat from it because the power he despises is real.

The problem with Milton's Lucifer is that he is not synonymous with the Lucifer of the Bible or the Lucifer of Christian tradition. He is a figment of Milton's heterodox imagination. Milton's God is not the Trinitarian God of the Christians but a Unitarian God whose Son is a mere creature, albeit the greatest of all creatures. Considering Milton's theological break with orthodoxy, his denial of the Trinity and, in consequence, his denial of the Incarnation also, it is grievously erroneous to see *Paradise Lost* as a Christian work. Except for its biblical trappings, it is no more Christian, in an orthodox sense, than the earlier epics of Homer and Virgil, and arguably less so. It might be argued, for instance, as we have done earlier in this book, that Homer and Virgil were groping in the right direction, toward the light of the Gospel, whereas Milton, rejecting the Church and the traditions of Christendom, was groping in the wrong direction, away from the light of the Gospel. Homer and Virgil might be seen as virgins awaiting the coming of the Bridegroom, whereas Milton is the disgruntled divorcé who turns his back on the marriage.

Regardless of whether William Blake was right when he said of Milton that he was "of the devil's party without knowing it",[1] Milton was indubitably doing the real

---

[1] William Blake, *The Marriage of Heaven and Hell* (Boston: John W. Luce, 1906), 11.

diabolus a service in inventing a mythical devil who has proved so attractive. Milton's Lucifer has what he perceives to be a just grievance and rebels against the perceived injustice with great courage. By way of contrast, it is hard to feel much sympathy with Milton's God, who is not loved because he is not loveable. He is an omnipotent Puritan prig who is right because of his might. A Pharisee himself, he might well have been the sort of God whom the Pharisees worshipped, but he has little in common with the God of the Christians. Meanwhile, Milton's Son is not worshipped because he is not God. In marked contrast to the biblical Jesus, he is depicted by Milton as a warrior who boasts of his martial prowess. It is little wonder that an atheist, such as Percy Bysshe Shelley, could claim that Milton's Satan was morally superior to his God. Perhaps nobody in history has done more to evoke sympathy for the devil than John Milton, even though we may presume that he would have been appalled at this dark side of his legacy.

In answer to the original provocative question, Milton's Lucifer is not Christian. He is no more Christian than the poet who gave him life. In consequence, those who feel that they have sympathy for the Miltonian devil are not sympathizing with the real Satan, any more than they are rebelling against the real Christ. They are merely pursuing the shadows of Milton's dark and unenlightened theology.

24

Gulliver's Travels

Jonathan Swift was born in Dublin of English parents in 1667, four years after Milton had finished writing *Paradise Lost*. Ordained as a minister of the Church of Ireland, he aligned himself with the High Church party at the Catholic end of the Protestant-Catholic spectrum in the Anglican church. His sympathies were very much on the side of tradition in an age subject to an accelerating charge toward modernity. In this sense, his is a "conservative" voice in the historical culture wars. Specifically, in the ongoing Quarrel of the Ancients and the Moderns that had been raging in France and then in England throughout the seventeenth century, Swift was a resolute proponent of the position of the Ancients. Along with his friend, the Catholic writer Alexander Pope, he represents the satirical reaction against scientolatry (the idolization of science as having all the necessary answers that human society needs) and chronological snobbery (the supercilious and arrogant dismissal of the past as being inexorably inferior to the present and the future), which are the defining characteristics of the Enlightenment. This needs to be borne in mind as we seek to unlock the nuances and subtleties of Swift's satirical commentary on contemporary culture in *Gulliver's Travels*.

As we begin reading this often misunderstood classic, it is crucial to remember that Swift is not Gulliver and that the protagonist of his satire does not act as a spokesman for Swift's own perspective. On the contrary, establishing a critical distance between the author and his fictional protagonist is absolutely necessary to a proper understanding of the meaning of the work. Swift creates Gulliver as the caricature of a stereotypical "modern" in order to satirize and ultimately lampoon the follies of the Enlightenment and its modernism and scientism. One wonders, in fact, if Swift chose the very name of Gulliver as a phonetic melding of the word "gull", which means a dupe or credulous person, and the word "traveler". Gulliver is the archetypal gullible traveler! Commenting on this critical distance between the author and his fictional protagonist, Dutton Kearney states in his introduction to the Ignatius Critical Edition of *Gulliver's Travels* that Swift is "the last of the Renaissance humanists", whereas Gulliver is "the first of the moderns".[1]

The work itself, which was published in 1726, is divided into four parts, each representing separate voyages that Gulliver undertakes: first, to Lilliput; second, to Brobdingnag; third, to Laputa, Balnibarbi, Luggnagg, Glubbdubdrib, and Japan; and finally, to the country of the Houyhnhnms. In general terms, Part I is a satire on politics and religion; Part II is a satire on the quarrel between the Ancients and the Moderns, including a satirical attack on the misanthropy of Thomas Hobbes; Part III is a satire on science, scientism, and notions of "progress"; and Part IV is a satire of Enlightenment philosophy. In the broadest sense, Swift satirizes the sin of pride in human and political relationships and highlights the limits of human reason, and how reason itself can be poisoned by pride. With respect to the latter, the division of rational beings into two types, the irrational emotion-driven

[1] Jonathan Swift, *Gulliver's Travels*, ed. Dutton Kearney, Ignatius Critical Editions (San Francisco: Ignatius Press, 2010), x.

yahoos and the rational emotionless houhnhnyms, serves as Swift's calling down of a plague on both the cynical materialism of Hobbes and the radical idealism of Descartes.

At the end of his travels, Gulliver is reduced to a misanthropic mess through his gullible adoption of Enlightenment philosophies, treating with cynical contempt the yahoos (Hobbesian man) and idolizing the emotionless idealism of the houyhnhnms (Cartesian man). Upon his return home, he treats his own wife and family with disgust, seeing them as being akin to the yahoos he met on his travels and considering them, like the yahoos, as nothing but bestial slaves of appetite.

In the midst of the madness caused by Gulliver's gullibility, Swift dexterously slips in the presence of sanity in the character of Don Pedro, who rescues Gulliver and brings him home to England for the final time. Don Pedro, a Catholic Christian, serves as the representative of a real human person and, therefore, as the antidote to the extremes of the Hobbesian and Cartesian understanding of man that had so confused Gulliver. It is the common sense and Christian charity of this representative of humanity that Gulliver should seek to imitate and emulate, not the theoretical and abstract idealism of the houyhnhnms. Gulliver does not learn the lesson that Don Pedro's presence and example teach, but surely the reader is meant to do so.

Once we are able to see the travels of Gulliver through the eyes of his sagacious creator and not through the gullible eyes of the traveler himself, we begin to glean the wisdom that *Gulliver's Travels* offers and can begin, therefore, to see that it is as relevant to our own times as it was to the times in which Swift wrote. It is not of an age but for all ages. Such perennial relevance is what marks *Gulliver's Travels* as belonging with the other great books of civilization. For this reason, it should be both celebrated and read.

25

Sense and Sensibility

Jane Austen is a giantess among giants, towering above the greatest writers of her own sex and indeed of both sexes. With the exception perhaps of Homer, Virgil, Dante, and Shakespeare, she holds her own among the greatest of all time. She can be mentioned in the same breath as the great Russian novelists Leo Tolstoy and Fyodor Dostoyevsky, as well as the American novelist Charles Dickens. Few indeed can hold a candle to her in terms of the sheer brilliance of her work and the perceptive depths that she fathoms. Like Shakespeare, she can be said to be not of an age but for all time.

Born in 1775, the daughter of an Anglican clergyman, Miss Austen entered a world that was ripe for, and would soon be rife with, revolution. The American Revolution was ushering into existence a new sort of nation, bereft of both monarchy and aristocracy, and the French Revolution in 1789 would bring down the *ancien régime*, replacing it with a secularist tyranny. Against these new ideas, Edmund Burke sounded a sagacious and cautionary note, especially in his *Reflections on the Revolution in France*, which was published at the end of 1790. Many of Burke's views can be seen to be represented in the character of Fanny Price in *Mansfield Park*, suggestive of Austen's own sympathy for Burke's anti-revolutionary position, and it might be suggested that

the hero's name, Edmund Bertram, is a phonetic allusion to
Edmund Burke himself, which would indicate that Burke
had been a mentor to the young Miss Austen as Bertram had
been a mentor to the young Miss Price.

As for Jane Austen's stance with respect to the Catholic Church, she was, like Burke, sympathetic to Catholicism at a time when anti-Catholic bigotry and sectarianism
was the default position in English culture. Although this
can be discerned implicitly in her novels, it was present
most obviously and emphatically in her juvenilia, especially
in the "History of England", which was written in 1791
when she was only fifteen years old. This "History" lampoons and satirizes the anti-Catholic stance of conventional
history books, especially Oliver Goldsmith's outrageously
"anti-papist" four-volume "history" of England. In stark
and remarkable contrast to the bias of Protestant history
that overlooked the tyranny of Tudor England, the teenage
Miss Austen depicts Elizabeth I as an unmitigated tyrant
and shows Mary, Queen of Scots, to be the martyred victim of Tudor tyranny. In supporting the Catholic Stuarts
against the anti-Catholic Tudors, she was countering the
prejudice of her times and was showing herself to be an
unwitting prophet of what would later become known as
Anglo-Catholicism. In this, as in so much else, Catholics
can feel entirely comfortable in the presence of the feminine genius of Jane Austen.

Perhaps the most frequently recurring theme in Austen's
work is a disdain for the irrational tenets of Romanticism,
which emphasized emotion and the feelings of the heart
over the reasoning of the head. From her earliest juvenile
writings, such as *Love and Freindship* (*sic*), written in 1790,
to her mature novels of more than twenty years later, she
lampoons the sort of Romantic novels in which women are
depicted as irrational beings, weak-willed and weak-minded.

Whereas her own novels contain such women, who commit the folly of following feeling in defiance of the demands of moral responsibility, her heroines attain the fullness of human dignity, subjecting themselves as eminently rational creatures to the goodness of virtue and the objectivity of truth. In this, she has been called an Aristotelian, quite correctly, but she could as easily be described as a Thomist insofar as she accepted and embraced Christian realism in an age of embryonic relativism. She is, therefore, a veritable giantess as a philosopher, in addition to her genius as a storyteller and her perspicacity as an observer of the human condition.

All of the foregoing is present in *Sense and Sensibility*, the first published of Jane Austen's novels, which wrestles with the conflict between the calculating and calculated "sense" of the Enlightenment and the impulsive emotional "sensibility" of Romanticism.

At the time of the novel's publication in 1811, Romanticism's reaction against the Enlightenment was all the rage. Heralded by the publication of *Lyrical Ballads* in 1798, a volume of poetry co-authored by William Wordsworth and Samuel Taylor Coleridge, English Romanticism sought to respond to the empiricism and scientism of the so-called Age of Reason with an emotion-driven engagement with beauty. On the one side, the head ruled the heart; on the other, the heart ruled the head. Both sides are present in *Sense and Sensibility*.

At one end of the spectrum are the characters who adhere to sense to such a degree that they banish sensibility. These are characters, such as John and Fanny Dashwood and Lucy Steel, who are cold and calculating in their relations with others, using their "sense" to serve their own materialistic and prideful purposes. At the other end of the spectrum are those who adhere to sensibility to such a degree that they ignore or denigrate the importance of sense. Characters on the "sensibility" end of the spectrum include Marianne Dashwood and the dashing John Willoughby, whose reckless emotion-driven romance ends in heartbreak. Those at either of these extremes are shown to be morally flawed. Those who employ sense to the exclusion of sensibility allow their heads to rule their hearts to such a degree that they become hard-hearted; those who follow sensibility to the exclusion of sense allow their hearts to rule their heads to such a degree that they lose their heads and break their hearts.

The characters who are truly virtuous are those who keep their sense and sensibility in healthy and harmonious balance, finding and then following the Aristotelian *via media* between the two extremes. Edward Ferrars and Marianne Dashwood achieve this moral equanimity eventually, learning from their mistakes, whereas Colonel Brandon and Elinor Dashwood seem always to possess such ethical poise and balance, in spite of the great trials and tribulations that they face. One suspects that the latter, the indomitably decorous and yet temperately passionate Miss Dashwood, bears a remarkable likeness to the indomitably decorous and beguilingly elusive Miss Austen. Indeed, it is through Jane Austen's heroines that we perceive the virtue and brilliance of the author herself, who always allowed her own sense and sensibility to be governed by her deep Christian faith.

26

Pride and Prejudice

In the first of her published novels, Jane Austen presents "sense" and "sensibility" as two ends of a spectrum. At the sense end of the spectrum, the head rules the heart to such an extent that the heart is hardened, losing its sensibility; at the sensibility end of the spectrum, the heart rules the head to such a degree that the losing of heads leads to the breaking of hearts. The characters who are truly virtuous are those who keep their sense and sensibility in healthy and harmonious balance, finding and then following the Aristotelian via media between the two extremes.

Although this understanding of sense and sensibility is present in all of Miss Austen's novels, the focus in the second of her novels, published in 1813, is the relationship between pride and prejudice. Whereas sense and sensibility can be separated, with disastrous consequences, pride and prejudice are always inseparable, the former always resulting in the latter. Such an understanding is a further manifestation of Miss Austen's Aristotelianism or, more specifically, her Thomism.

St. Thomas Aquinas teaches that the perception of reality is dependent on the virtue of humility. It is humility that bestows the sense of gratitude that opens the eyes in wonder, and it is only when the eyes are wide open in wonder that the soul is moved to the contemplation that is necessary for its dilation (*dilatatio*) into the fullness of reality. The absence of humility is pride, which lacks gratitude and closes the eyes to any sense of wonder, rendering contemplation and dilation unattainable. In short and in sum, those with pride are always prejudiced because they are blind to the fullness of reality. It is this understanding of pride and its blindness that animates *Pride and Prejudice*.

Elizabeth Bennet and Mr. Darcy are blinded by their pride into forming prejudiced presumptions about each other. It is only as they gain humility that each is able to see the other more perceptively. Elizabeth, for instance, is predisposed to believe Mr. Wickham's lies about Mr. Darcy because of her prejudiced appraisal of the latter's character. She is "absolutely ashamed of herself" when she finally realizes that she has been "blind, partial, prejudiced, absurd".[1] The realization is a revelation, enabling her to see herself from a fresh perspective. Her pride having been humiliated, she attains the humility that is necessary to see herself more clearly. Indeed, she sees herself for the first time: "Till this moment, I never knew myself."[2]

Mr. Darcy, on the other hand, needs to learn condescension in the humble and not the prideful sense of the word. He must cease looking down upon the comparatively low-born Elizabeth and needs to descend from his high horse, not merely in order to meet her eye-to-eye but to descend further, onto his knees, that he might look up to her in reverence and with a love that knows it is not worthy. Such a sense of unworthiness animates his confession to Elizabeth of his earlier ill-treatment of her: "The recollection of what I then said, of my conduct, my

[1] Jane Austen, *Pride and Prejudice*, ed. Joseph Pearce, Ignatius Critical Editions (San Francisco: Ignatius Press, 2008), 207.
[2] Ibid.

manners, my expressions during the whole of it, is now, and has been many months, inexpressibly painful to me. Your reproof, so well applied ... You know not, you can scarcely conceive, how they have tortured me;—though it was some time, I confess, before I was reasonable enough to allow their justice."[3]

It is only through learning to show reverence and respect for others that we are able to love them and, through such love, know them as they are. It is in this way that Elizabeth and Darcy grow in virtue. Their sacrificing of themselves in love enables each to draw the other toward the humble demands of the undeserved gift of love: conversion, confession, and forgiveness. It is, therefore, through the love of another that we are able to gain the maturity that comes through moral formation and growth, a maturity that is necessary for the sustenance of loving relationships and the attainment of happiness.

Apart from the axiomatic theme that gives the novel its title, other important themes are also present. As Christopher Blum notes in his introduction to the Ignatius Critical Edition of the novel, *Pride and Prejudice* is a reflection on "love, marriage, family, and the search for stability and goodness in community".[4] Since marriage provides the very framework and fabric of the moral life of society, healthy marriages are necessary, not merely for the individual happiness of the spouses but for the common good of society itself. In this sense, *Pride and Prejudice* serves as a timely witness to the need for the traditional family at a time when all aspects of family life are under relentless attack.

Perhaps the final words on this most popular of novels should be left to Miss Austen herself. In an evening prayer

[3] Ibid., 358.
[4] Ibid., ix.

that she is believed to have composed, she beseeches the most merciful God to "save us from deceiving ourselves by Pride or Vanity".[5] In the case of Miss Elizabeth Bennet and Mr. Darcy, this prayer is answered.

[5] For the textual history of this and other prayers attributed to her, see Jane Austen, *Catharine and Other Writings*, eds. Margaret Anne Doody and Douglas Murray (Oxford, UK: Oxford University Press, 1993), 283–84; Bruce Stovel, "'A Nation Improving in Religion': Jane Austen's Prayers and Their Place in Her Life and Art", *Persuasions: A Publication of the Jane Austen Society of North America*, 16 (1994): 185–86.

27

Frankenstein

Mary Shelley's *Frankenstein* is one of the most influential novels of the nineteenth century and one of the most confused and confusing. Containing a maelstrom of conflicting forces, it expresses the whirlwind of warring influences within the mind and heart of its teenage author. On a purely emotional level, the young Mary Shelley was surrounded by tragedy as she wrote the novel, including the death in early infancy of her first child and the suicide of two intimate relations, the death of one of whom must have weighed heavily on her conscience. She was also battling with the monsters of modernity and struggling with the atheistic philosophy of her father and the iconoclastic musings of her lover. In addition, within the pages of *Frankenstein* we see the savagery of Rousseau; the pseudo-satanic manipulation of Milton; the Romantic reaction against the "dark satanic mills" of scientism and industrialism; the conflict between the "light" Romanticism of Wordsworth and Coleridge and the "darker" Romanticism of Byron and Shelley; and, perhaps most enigmatically, the struggle between the two Shelleys themselves and the emergence of Mary from Percy's shadow.

Mary began writing *Frankenstein* in June 1816, when she was still only eighteen years old, and would not finish it until the following May. Although the tragic backdrop of her private life pervades the whole work, it should not eclipse the many other elements that serve to add to the deadly cocktail of depth and delusion that makes *Frankenstein* such a beguilingly deceptive story.

In giving *Frankenstein* the alternative title of *The Modern Prometheus* and coupling it with the epigraph conveying Adam's complaint from *Paradise Lost*, we are given tantalizing clues concerning the aesthetic and philosophical roots of Mary Shelley's inspiration and perhaps an inkling of her purpose. Prometheus presumes to take powers that are not rightfully his in order to create man; Adam presumes to rebuke his Creator for bringing him into existence. It is clear, therefore, that Victor Frankenstein can be seen as a Prometheus figure, and the Monster as a figure of Milton's Adam. It is important from the outset, however, to distinguish between the biblical Adam and the Adam depicted by Milton in *Paradise Lost*. The two Adams are very different, and it is perilous to conflate them. The biblical Adam does not rebuke his Creator for bringing him into existence. He never takes the prideful position of questioning the Creator's wisdom in creating him; still less does he imply the nihilistic option of wishing his own oblivion. It is, therefore, a peculiar Miltonian "Christianity" that serves as a catalyst to Mary Shelley's fevered imagination.

The impact of the monstrous imagination of Milton on the writing of *Frankenstein* is matched in importance by the "savage" ideas of Jean-Jacques Rousseau. The ideas in Rousseau's *Emile* resonate clearly with the Monster's "education", leading to the Monster's echoing Rousseau in his conclusion, from history, that man poisons everything he touches. Cast in the role of Rousseau's noble savage, the Monster sits in judgment over the decadence of "civilized" humanity.

The connection with the noble savagery of Rousseau brands Mary Shelley as a literary luddite. Like the literal luddites who were her exact contemporaries (the luddite riots taking place from 1812 to 1818), she distrusted science and the encroachments of industrialism. She was at one with the earlier generation of Romantics, such as Blake, Coleridge, and Wordsworth, who wrote disparagingly of the "dark satanic mills" of the newly emergent industrial conurbations.

The final and most fascinating facet of *Frankenstein* is the extent of Percy Shelley's influence on the work, and the extent to which the novel can be read as Mary Shelley's emergence from the poet's pervasive shadow. The idealized or romanticized Romantic poet, as represented in the novel by the faithful Clerval, has much more in common with the tradition-oriented and profoundly Christian Romanticism of Wordsworth and Coleridge, or even with Sir Walter Scott, than with the iconoclastic "futurism" and dark egocentrism of Percy Shelley. Clerval's "favourite study consisted in books of chivalry and romance", and Frankenstein recalls nostalgically that "when very young, I can remember, that we used to act plays composed by him out of these favourite books, the principal characters of which were Orlando, Robin Hood, Amadis, and St George".[1] Clerval, therefore, is presented as a neo-medievalist who gains his inspiration not from "the gigantic shadows which futurity casts upon the present", as Percy Shelley proclaimed in his "Defense of Poetry",[2] but from the traditional and romantic shadows of the past.

[1] Mary Shelley, *Frankenstein*, ed. Joseph Pearce, Ignatius Critical Editions (San Francisco: Ignatius Press, 2008), 28.

[2] Percy Bysshe Shelley, "A Defense of Poetry", in *The Complete Works of Percy Bysshe Shelley*, vol. 7 (London: Ernest Benn, 1965), 140.

Frankenstein states that "in Clerval I saw the image of my former self",[3] indicating that he had once shared the blessed serenity of Clerval's Romanticism but had slipped through pride into darkness and into a darker vision of reality. Clerval is, along with Elizabeth, the most unambiguously and sympathetically portrayed character in the whole novel and is, at the same time, the antithesis of Percy Shelley's ideal poet.

Mary Shelley's sympathy with the Romanticism of Wordsworth and Coleridge is illustrated in *Frankenstein* by the repeated references to Coleridge's *The Rime of the Ancient Mariner*. At the beginning of the novel, in Captain Walton's second letter to his sister, he quotes from Coleridge's poem and states, reassuringly, that since he will "kill no albatross"[4] she need not fear for his safety. In *The Rime of the Ancient Mariner*, a profoundly Christian allegory, the killing of the albatross is symbolic of sin and the taboo attached to the sinful act, and there is a clear connection between the crime of Coleridge's Mariner and the crime of Mary Shelley's Frankenstein. In each case, the misguided protagonist ignores the taboo, taking the Promethean or satanic option and paying the consequences of so doing. This is made even more apparent when Coleridge's poem is quoted again, immediately after Frankenstein has brought the Monster to life.

The Monster is described as being "demoniacal" and as "a thing such as even Dante could not have conceived".[5] It is evident from these intertextual references that Mary is working on the level not merely of physics but of metaphysics. The Monster is not a mere product of science

[3] Shelley, *Frankenstein*, 151.
[4] Ibid., 16.
[5] Ibid., 50.

but is the consequence of satanic choice. It is not only monstrous, like Godzilla or King Kong, but demonic, like Satan and his servants, though the sympathy we feel for the hapless Monster reflects a Miltonian conception of the satanic. Mary Shelley's work transcends the physical limitations of Percy Shelley's gloomy and narrow atheism and enters the infinite and eternal realm of religion, making the leap from the finite to the infinite with the chosen assistance of two of the most profoundly Christian poets Coleridge and Dante.

The traditional morality at the heart of Mary Shelley's vision is made even more apparent through the words of the character Elizabeth. "Everyone adored Elizabeth",[6] we are told when she is first introduced, and she is depicted thereafter as a gentle-hearted soul. She might be seen, within the broader context of the novel, as Mary's presentation of the idealized or perfect woman, as her Beatrice, just as Clerval is her presentation of the idealized or perfect poet.

With adept feminine finesse and an adroitness of touch, Elizabeth seeks to draw Frankenstein away from his pride and morbidity in order to restore him to spiritual health, much as Clerval's love had restored him to physical health. It is evident that Elizabeth upholds conventional moral values; and the fact that she is cast in the role of a sane and saintly heroine, and later as an innocent victim, in contrast to the mad and evil actions of Frankenstein and the Monster, suggests that we are meant to sympathize with the values she espouses, such as her praise of farming, with its "healthy happy life".[7]

The irony of Mary Shelley's most celebrated novel is that it appears to be animated by the author's longing for a

[6] Ibid., 27.
[7] Ibid., 55.

"healthy happy life" that was very different from the miserable suicide-haunted life she was living when the novel was written. Percy Shelley's iconoclastic pursuit of "freedom", made manifest in his elopement with Mary and the suicide of his wife which was its consequence, was the dark inspirational backdrop to the novel's underlying sense of desperation. Mary Shelley seems to have learned the hard way that iconoclastic "freedoms" do not make men into gods, or women into goddesses, but that they turn men into monsters and women into their victims. Understood in this context, *Frankenstein* is an expression of lost innocence, sacrificed on the altar of Promethean promiscuity, screaming to be liberated from its "liberation".

28

The Betrothed

If the greatest masterpiece of Italian literature, Dante's *Divine Comedy*, could realistically be acclaimed as the greatest poem ever written, the other great masterpiece of Italian literature, *The Betrothed* (*I Promessi Sposi*) by Alessandro Manzoni, could be acclaimed as the greatest-ever novel. This latter claim will come as a surprise to those who might not even have heard of Manzoni's classic work. And yet, in spite of the relative neglect it has suffered, it rivals *Don Quixote*, *Pride and Prejudice*, *A Tale of Two Cities*, *War and Peace*, *The Brothers Karamazov*, and any other claimants to literary preeminence. Such an appraisal of its merit would certainly accord with the view of most Italians, who are baffled by the relative lack of recognition that Manzoni's magnum opus has received globally. It forms an indispensable part of the curriculum in Italian high schools, and Manzoni's embrace of the Florentine dialect in his writing of *The Betrothed* helped to establish and formalize the modern Italian language. Furthermore, as a work that is more accessible than *The Divine Comedy*, it is the most widely read of all works of Italian literature and, with the exception of Dante's *Commedia*, the most widely critiqued and scrutinized by scholars.

Alessandro Manzoni was a revert to the practice of the Catholic faith, having wandered off as a young man in pursuit of the fashionable and anti-Catholic secularism espoused by the followers of Voltaire. Having returned to the Catholic faith with a renewed vigor and fervor, he began writing religious poetry and authored a scholarly treatise on Catholic morality. It was, therefore, as a devout Catholic that Manzoni set to work on *The Betrothed*, his own muse being betrothed to the essential truths that the novel radiates.

First published in 1827 in three volumes and later, in 1842, in a revised definitive version, *The Betrothed* is a historical novel recounting events from two centuries earlier. At the heart of the story is the agonizing relationship of Renzo and Lucia, the betrothed couple, who are swept apart by political intrigue and circumstance. It follows the hapless pair in their seemingly hopeless quest to be reunited, a storyline that will remind American readers of Longfellow's *Evangeline*. Against the backdrop of petty tyranny and political turmoil, and amid the mayhem of revolutionary mobs and the miasma of plague-ridden streets, the story of the lovers is interwoven with the stories of great sinners and even greater saints. Its greatest strength, however, is the menagerie of multifarious characters that Manzoni presents to the reader, a motley medley of all that is best and worst in humanity, much as Chaucer presents to the reader in the General Prologue to the *Canterbury Tales*. A brief depiction of the most important of these will provide a picture, a character portrait, of the novel itself.

Lucia is a worthy heroine in the tradition of great literary heroines. She reminds us of Homer's Penelope in her faithful fortitude in the midst of great trials and tribulations, exhibiting saintly spiritual strength in the very heart of the darkness in which she all too often finds herself. Like Penelope, she is besieged by the unwelcome advances of wicked men and beset by troubles that are not of her own making. She exhibits the powerful silence of Shakespeare's Cordelia in her resolve to refrain from the path of least resistance, retaining her virtue in the midst of viciousness. In so doing, she also reminds us of Dante's Beatrice insofar as she represents a very icon of idealized femininity, worthy of anyone's love and warranting great sacrifice on the part of the lover in the quest to win her hand. Renzo is as utterly unworthy of her as Dante is of Beatrice. He is hotheaded, rash in his judgments, and rushed in his actions. His lack of prudence and temperance all too often makes matters worse. And yet, in spite of his weaknesses, he is good and stouthearted and is lacking in neither courage nor cunning. For this reason, the reader can't help liking him, in spite of his infuriating lack of judgment. We wish him well, and wish him success in being reunited with the woman of whom he is so evidently the inferior.

In Don Abbondio and Fra Cristoforo, we are shown the worst and the best in the priesthood and the religious life, much as Chaucer shows us the worst and the best in presenting us with the Friar and the Parson. Don Abbondio is craven in his abandonment of Renzo and Lucia to the wickedness of Don Rodrigo, placing his own self-interest and material comfort over the good of his flock. In contrast, Fra Cristoforo is fearless in his pursuit of justice for the betrothed couple, striding into the very lion's den in order to confront Don Rodrigo.

In Don Rodrigo and the Unnamed (L'Innominato), Manzoni presents us with two fearsome tyrants, each of whom has tyrannized the weak in the wielding of power for his own self-serving purposes. In the latter, he also shows us one of the most powerful and palpable examples of spiritual conversion in all of literature, a conversion that was based on the real-life conversion of Francesco Bernardino Visconti.

Two other characters based upon real-life historical figures are Federico Borromeo and the Nun of Monza. The former, a cousin of St. Charles Borromeo, followed his kinsman as Cardinal Archbishop of Milan, as well as following in his kinsman's saintly footsteps as a holy servant of the Church, tireless and courageous in his zeal for souls. Manzoni is dexterous in his portrayal of Borromeo's sanctity, relating it with masculine matter-of-factness without ever stooping to the saccharine level of the hagiographic. The Nun of Monza, on the other hand, is based upon a real-life noblewoman who, having been coerced into a religious order by her family, lives an embittered life, succumbing to the sin of fornication and its sordid ramifications. The fact that the pure and chaste Lucia is entrusted to the care of such a woman adds one more agonizing twist and turn to this most anguished of tales.

Apart from these leading players, a number of minor characters add their own inimitable *je ne sais pas quoi* to the story. The most memorable of these is Dr. Azzeccagarbugli, whose surname is rendered by the novel's translator as Dr. Quibbleweaver, which, aside from being quintessentially and delightfully Dickensian, is an apt appendage for a corrupt lawyer who weaves quibbles into hard cash for himself and his rich and equally corrupt clients.

One final aspect of Manzoni's novel needs to be mentioned. The whole work is imbued with good humor, itself an expression of the author's goodness, which alleviates the grimness of the novel's gravitas with the levitas of Christian hope. The narrative voice of the author, when it interjects itself into the story, is one that lightens and leavens the whole work with whimsy. It is the presence of the author's overarching and overriding Christian vision that trumpets a note of triumph and even triumphalism into the darkest corners of the narrative. Irrespective of each ensuing catastrophic turn in events, one always senses in the gentle intrusion of the authorial voice that all will be well in the end. It doesn't matter how bad things are or how much worse they become. Even in the midst of the madness of the Machiavel or the massacre of the innocents, there is always the promise of final victory. It is the very essence of great Christian literature, which always sees the silver lining to every cloud, and the unseen sun that it signifies, knowing that the darkest of tragedies is always and ultimately subject to the divinest of comedies.

29

Wuthering Heights

Emily Brontë was the daughter of an ordained minister of the Church of England, who served his parish devoutly and diligently for forty years. Like her father, Emily was a faithful and devout Christian, a fact that is evident in the moral perspective manifested in her famous novel *Wuthering Heights*.

The darkness of the novel is driven by the refusal of the novel's principal protagonists to love their neighbors or to forgive those who have sinned against them. The result is a destructive chain reaction in which more and more innocent lambs are turned into vengeful wolves. This is the very animus of the novel and the impetus of its plot.

The light of Christianity penetrates the darkness of the novel in the words and actions of Nelly Dean. It is she who attempts to bring the plot's protagonists to their senses. She warns Heathcliff that "proud people breed sad sorrows for themselves".[1] These words of wisdom will serve as the very defining moral and motto of the novel. The whole story is the weaving of the sad sorrows brought upon the main protagonists by their own pride.

The wisdom of Nelly's words and the suspicion that they are the words of the author speaking vicariously are present

[1] Emily Brontë, *Wuthering Heights*, ed. Joseph Pearce, Ignatius Critical Editions (San Francisco: Ignatius Press, 2008), 66.

133

in an exchange with Catherine in which Nelly emerges as an incisive Christian theologian. "If I were in heaven," Catherine says, "I should be extremely miserable."[2] The reason, says Nelly, is because "all sinners would be miserable in heaven."[3] Her axiomatic riposte should be borne in mind as the dialogue continues, particularly in the light, or darkness, of Catherine's obsession with Heathcliff:

> My great miseries in this world have been Heathcliff's miseries, and I watched and felt each from the beginning; my great thought in living is himself. If all perished, and *he* remained, I should still continue to be; and, if all else remained, and he were annihilated, the Universe would turn to a mighty stranger. I should not seem a part of it. . . . My love for Heathcliff resembles the eternal rocks ... a source of little visible delight, but necessary. Nelly, I *am* Heathcliff—he's always, always in my mind—not as a pleasure, any more than I am always a pleasure to myself—but, say my own being—so don't talk of our separation again.[4]

In this well-known passage, Catherine is confessing the infernal nature of her "love" for Heathcliff, who is not merely her idol but her demonic god. She not only worships him; she is possessed by him. This demonic dimension was not lost on G.K. Chesterton, who wrote that Heathcliff "fails as a man as catastrophically as he succeeds as a demon".[5] The demonic is further suggested by the fact that Catherine's words, "I *am* Heathcliff", echo those of Milton's Satan, "myself am hell".[6] Like Satan she is

---

[2] Ibid., 92.

[3] Ibid.

[4] Ibid., 94–95 (italics in original).

[5] G.K. Chesterton, *The Victorian Age in Literature* (London: Williams & Norgate, 1913), 113.

[6] John Milton, *Paradise Lost*, bk. 4, line 75.

exiled from heaven because everywhere, even heaven, would be "a mighty stranger" to her if Heathcliff were not there; she would "not seem a part of it". She would rather be with him in hell than without him in heaven. Nothing will separate her from the "love" of her god, not even the love of God. She will be with Heathcliff forever, not merely "till death do us part" but beyond death itself. Heathcliff is the "eternal rock" upon which she builds her church. He is "a source of little visible delight" but, on the contrary, is "darkness visible",[7] like Milton's Satan, and the source of all her suffering. Yet she will not be separated from the hell she has chosen. She gets what she chooses. This is profoundly orthodox Christian theology, in the finest tradition of Dante's *Inferno*.

The towering influence of Dante is once more evident in the scene between Heathcliff and Catherine when the latter is on her deathbed. Catherine's "love" for Heathcliff is so disordered that it seems indistinguishable from hate. "I shall not pity you, not I", she says. "You have killed me—and thriven on it, I think."[8] The moment of death, for Heathcliff and for Catherine, is not a time for reconciliation, either with God or with each other. It is a time for bitter reproach, a time for venting one's spleen in one final act of self-destructive abandonment. "I wish I could hold you ... till we were both dead!" Catherine exclaims. "I shouldn't care what you suffered. I care nothing for your sufferings. Why shouldn't you suffer? I do!"[9]

Catherine still has no desire for heaven, preferring the hell of Heathcliff. She makes her choice and is self-condemned by it. Heathcliff, for his part, spits his venom

[7] Ibid., bk. 1, line 63.
[8] Brontë, *Wuthering Heights*, 178.
[9] Ibid.

at Catherine but would prefer to writhe with her in the inferno, in an eternal love-hate embrace, than live without her in heaven or on earth:

> "Are you *possessed with a devil*," he pursued, savagely, "to talk in that manner to me, when you are dying? Do you reflect that all those words will be branded in my memory, and *eating deeper eternally*, after you have left me? ... It is not sufficient for your *infernal selfishness*, that while you are at peace *I shall writhe in the torments of hell*?"
> "*I shall not be at peace*," moaned Catherine.[10]

The emphasis has been added to highlight the metaphysical drama that lurks beneath the physical surface of their exchange. For Emily, as for her great forebear and inspiration, Dante, every act in life has eternal significance.

In stark contrast to the benign Christian presence of Nelly is the malign presence of Joseph, the puritanical and moralizing Calvinist. Joseph represents the superficial Christian. He's not the real thing. His lack of charity disqualifies him. Echoing Christ's condemnation of the scribe, the Pharisee, and the hypocrite, Emily is following in a noble tradition of Christian literature in exposing the hypocrisy of uncharitable Christians. Dante has a whole section (*bowge*) of the eighth circle of hell reserved especially for the hypocrites, and Chaucer spends much of his General Prologue exposing the hypocrisy of many of his pilgrims.

The novel ends on a light note, in both senses of the word. Following Heathcliff's death, the darkness lifts and the emergent light lightens the burden of evil that has loomed, doom-laden, over the whole work. As Mr. Lockwood returns to Wuthering Heights, we are almost

[10] Ibid., 179 (italics added).

dazzled by light and lifted by light-heartedness. Love is in the air—true love, not its infernal inversion. This happy ending serves as the final judgment on the novel itself, confirming that Emily Brontë, like the indomitable Nelly Dean, is on the side of the angels.

30

A Christmas Carol

Originally published in 1843, Dickens' ghost story, *A Christmas Carol*, is one of the most popular works of literature ever written. Its mean-spirited protagonist, Ebenezer Scrooge, stands out from Dickens' imaginary menagerie of characters as a cautionary icon of miserly worldliness but also as a beacon of hope and redemption, as powerful parabolically as the prodigal son of which he is a type.

The story begins with the cold hard fact that Jacob Marley is "as dead as a door-nail":

> There is no doubt that Marley was dead. This must be distinctly understood, or nothing wonderful can come of the story I am going to relate. If we were not perfectly convinced that Hamlet's Father died before the play began, there would be nothing more remarkable in his taking a stroll at night, in an easterly wind, upon his own ramparts, than there would be in any other middle-aged gentleman rashly turning out after dark in a breezy spot ... literally to astonish his son's weak mind.[1]

The connection with *Hamlet* at the very beginning of the novella has a deep significance that the whimsical tone

---

[1] Charles Dickens, *A Christmas Carol: A Ghost Story of Christmas* (London: Chapman & Hall, 1843; Project Gutenberg, 2018), stave 2, "Marley's Ghost", https://www.gutenberg.org/files/46/46-h/46-h.htm.

should not obscure. In Shakespeare's play as in Dickens' story, the ghosts serve to introduce not merely a supernatural dimension to the work but a supernatural perception of reality. The ghosts reveal what is hidden to mortal eyes. They see more. They serve as supernatural messengers who reveal crimes that would otherwise have remained hidden. Their intervention is necessary for reality to be seen and understood and for justice to be done. Thus, in connecting Jacob Marley's ghost to the ghost of Hamlet's father, Dickens is indicating the role and purpose of the ghosts that he will introduce to Scrooge, and to us. They will show us not only Scrooge but ourselves in a manner that has the power to surprise us out of our own worldliness and to open us to the spiritual realities that we are prone to forget.

It is, however, not only the ghosts who teach us timely and timeless lessons but our mortal neighbors also. It is, after all, worth remembering that the first visitors that Scrooge receives are not ghosts but men. His nephew waxes lyrical on what might be termed the magic or miracle of Christmas:

> I have always thought of Christmas time, when it has come round—apart from the veneration due to its sacred name and origin, if anything belonging to it can be apart from that—as a good time; a kind, forgiving, charitable, pleasant time; the only time I know of, in the long calendar of the year, when men and women seem by one consent to open their shut-up hearts freely, and to think of people below them as if they really were fellow-passengers to the grave, and not another race of creatures bound on other journeys.[2]

[2] Ibid.

There is no need to remind Scrooge's nephew of the necessity of keeping Christ in Christmas! He knows that it is venerated because of its sacred name, *Christ-Mass*, and because of its sacred origin in the birth of the Savior. How can anything associated with Christmas be separated from its sacred source and purpose? The very thought, as expressed in the nephew's afterthought, is plainly absurd. Scrooge, ironically, does not disagree. He has no intention of celebrating the feast while ignoring its sacred name and origin as do most people in our own hedonistic times. He does not want to celebrate it at all. After complaining that his nephew should let him keep Christmas in his own way, the nephew reminds him that he doesn't keep it at all. "Let me leave it alone, then",[3] Scrooge replies.

The other facet of the nephew's defense of Christmas that should not go unnoticed or unheeded is his reminder to his uncle that the poor and destitute are "fellow-passengers to the grave, and not another race of creatures bound on other journeys". This is not merely a memento mori, which, for the Christian, should always be a reminder of the Four Last Things—death, judgment, heaven, and hell—but is a reminder that we are not *homo sapiens*, smug in the presumption of our cleverness, but *homo viator*, creatures or "passengers" on the journey of life, the only purpose of which is to get to heaven. Furthermore, our fellow travelers, sanctified by their being made in God's image, are our mystical equals, irrespective of their social or economic status, whom we are commanded to love. They are not "another race of creatures bound on other journeys" but are our very kith and kin bound on the same journey of life as we are. The inescapable truth, inextricably bound to the great commandment of Christ that

---

[3] Ibid.

we love the Lord our God and that we love our neighbor (see Mt 22:37–38), is that we cannot reach the destination that is the very purpose of life's journey without helping our fellow travelers get there with us. The lesson that *A Christmas Carol* teaches is that our lives are not *owned* by us but are *owed* to another to whom the debt must be paid in the currency of self-sacrifice, which is love's means of exchange.

A Christmas Carol is, therefore, as might be expected of a meditation on the spirit of Christmas, a literary work that operates most profoundly on the level of theology. This is seen most clearly in the roles played by the various ghosts.

Marley's ghost, like the ghost of Hamlet's father, is apparently a soul in purgatory and not one of the damned. This is clear from its penitential and avowedly Christian spirit and its desire to save Scrooge from following in its folly-laden footsteps. When Scrooge seeks to console him with the reminder that he had always been "a good man of business", Marley's ghost wrings its hands in conscience-driven agitation. "Business!" he cries. "Mankind was my business. The common welfare was my business; charity, mercy, forbearance, and benevolence, were all my business. The dealings of my trade were but a drop of water in the comprehensive ocean of my business!"[4]

If Marley's ghost is the spirit of a mortal man, suffering penitentially and purgatorially for its sins, the Ghosts of Christmases Past, Present, and Yet to Come are best described as angels. They are divine messengers (*angelos*, in Greek, means "messenger"). More specifically, they might be seen as Scrooge's own guardian angels, as can be seen from the first Ghost's description of himself as being not the Ghost of Long Past but that of Scrooge's own past.

[4] Ibid.

The final aspect of *A Christmas Carol* that warrants mention, especially in light of its poignant pertinence to our own meretricious times, is its celebration of life in general and the lives of large families in particular. The burgeoning family of Bob Cratchit—in spite of its poverty, or dare we say because of it—is the very hearth and home from which the warmth of life and love glows through the pages of Dickens' story. At the very heart of that hearth and home is the blessed life of the disabled child, Tiny Tim, which shines forth in Tiny Tim's love for others and in the love that his family has for him. His very presence is the light of caritas that serves catalytically to bring Scrooge to his senses. After his conversion, Scrooge no longer sees the poor and disabled as being surplus to the needs of the population who should be allowed to die—as in our own day they are routinely killed or culled in the womb—but as a blessing to be cherished and praised. For this love of life, even of the life of the disabled, *especially* of the life of the disabled, is at the heart of everyone who knows the true spirit of Christmas as exemplified in the helplessness of the Babe of Bethlehem. "And so, as Tiny Tim observed, God bless Us, Every One!"[5]

[5] Ibid., stave 5, "The End of It".

31

A Tale of Two Cities

It could be argued and has been argued that, after Shake-speare, Charles Dickens is the finest writer in the English language. His works have forged their way into the canon to such a degree that it is much more difficult to know which of his novels to leave off the recommended reading list than it is to choose which to include. Each of us has his favorites, and each invariably begs to differ with his neighbor's choice. Does *David Copperfield* deserve pride of place, or *Nicholas Nickleby*, *Oliver Twist*, *Great Expectations*, or *Bleak House*? Who can possibly know which is Dick-ens' greatest work? It's a mystery as insoluble as that sur-rounding Edwin Drood in Dickens' last, unfinished work. Irrespective of such differences in opinion, *A Tale of Two Cities* wins the accolade as the most popular in terms of sales because, alongside *Don Quixote*, it is usually listed as the bestselling novel of all time, with sales exceeding two hundred million.

Published in 1858 and set in the two cities of London and Paris, the novel covers the years from 1757 to 1794, against the backdrop of the revolutionary fervor in France. Dickens' principal historical source was *The French Revolution: A History* by Thomas Carlyle, the revised edition of which was published in 1857. Much of the action is centered on some of the most horrific moments of the revolution, such as the storming of the Bastille in July 1789, the September Massacres of 1792, and the Reign of Terror in 1793 and 1794.

The symbolic scene is set in Saint Antoine, a poor suburb of Paris, when a wine cask drops to the street and smashes open, emptying its contents and spilling the bloodred liquid on the streets. This causes a frenzied scene of debauchery as men and women rush to drink and scoop up the pools of wine. As if to make the metaphor more obvious and inescapable, a solitary figure dips his finger in the spilled wine and writes the word "blood" on a nearby wall, prophesying the coming of revolution. The bloodthirsty image also serves to introduce the sadistically vengeful figures of Monsieur and Madame Defarge, who epitomize the bloodlustful hatred of the revolutionaries.

At the other end of the sociopolitical spectrum is the haughty and superciliously arrogant aristocrat, the Marquis St. Evrémonde. Ordering his carriage to be driven recklessly through a poor neighborhood, it strikes and kills a child. With his customary arrogance and contempt for the poor, the Marquis tosses a few coins to the child's bereft father and orders the carriage to drive on. When one of his coins is thrown back into the carriage, he curses the vulgarity of the common people, showing no sign of remorse for the life he has just taken. As the scene unfolds, the figure of Madame Defarge sits quietly, knitting patiently, biding her time. It's as though she represents in her very malevolence the silent presence of the diabolical vengeance that waits to be unleashed.

At the broken heart of the novel is the pathetic presence of Sydney Carton, drunk and dejected, moody and melancholy, who falls hopelessly in love with Lucie Manette. His love is literally hopeless and doomed to be unrequited because Lucie loves and marries the mysterious Frenchman

Charles Darnay. The two men bear a remarkable physical likeness to each other so that Carton is almost his rival's doppelgänger. Carton confesses his love for Lucie, simultaneously confessing his own dissolute listlessness and unworthiness. He promises to leave her in peace, thanking her for the joy she has given him, and then makes a prophetic promise that introduces the Christian theme of self-sacrificial love as the antidote to the world's arrogance, hatred, and spirit of vengeance: "I would embrace any sacrifice for you and for those dear to you."[1]

Against this spirit of Christlike love is the vengeful and malevolent spirit of Madame Defarge, who has been tirelessly knitting the names of those who must die when the revolution comes, an act that serves metaphorically as the weaving of her murderous web. It's as though she were a spider, a black widow, awaiting the time when she can enmesh those she hates, devouring them to assuage her insatiable appetite for blood. Her moment arrives with the storming of the Bastille when the mob unleashes its pent-up hatred. The streets of Saint Antoine, which had previously run red with spilled wine, now run red with blood, an infernal transubstantiation.

Charles Darnay is arrested for being the aristocratic nephew of the hated Marquis St. Evrémonde but is acquitted when it is revealed that he had renounced his title because of his uncle's cruelty toward the poor. He is, however, re-arrested and sentenced to death. Meanwhile, the hapless Carton walks the streets of Paris, haunted by his love of Lucie but also by the words spoken at his own father's funeral: "I am the resurrection and the life, saith the Lord: he that believeth in me, though he were dead,

---

[1] Charles Dickens, *A Tale of Two Cities*, ed. Michael D. Aeschliman, Ignatius Critical Editions (San Francisco: Ignatius Press, 2012), 175.

yet shall he live: and whosoever liveth and believeth in me, shall never die."[2]

Intent on saving Darnay, the man who had married the woman he loves, Carton contrives a way of taking Darnay's place, using his striking resemblance to the condemned man to fool the jailers. As he goes to his death the following morning, he is recognized by a poor woman who is also condemned to die. "Are you dying for him?", she asks. "And his wife and child", he replies.[3] The woman, overcome by his self-sacrificial love, asks to hold his "brave hand".[4] As he approaches the guillotine, Carton is encouraged by the thought of Lucie and Darnay raising a family. He then utters the concluding words of the novel: "It is a far, far better thing that I do, than I have ever done; it is a far, far better rest that I go to than I have ever known."[5]

Ironically but also divinely symmetrically, the book ends as it had begun with the imagery of resurrection from the dead. The first part of the book is entitled "Recalled to Life", an allusion to the fact that Lucie's father, who was thought to be dead, had been discovered to be alive. At the novel's conclusion, the dissolutely desolate Carton, the miserable good-for-nothing, is also "recalled to life". This time, however, it is not merely a resurrection from death to life, like Lazarus, but a resurrection from death to everlasting life, like Christ. Seldom has a novel had a happier ending.

[2] Ibid., 358. See Jn 11:25–26 (KJV).
[3] Ibid., 404.
[4] Ibid.
[5] Ibid., 428.

32

The Picture of Dorian Gray

Oscar Wilde wrote several first-rate plays, on which his literary reputation principally rests, and a number of mostly
second-rate poems. He is also lauded, quite rightly, for
his short stories, mainly for children, of which "The Selfish Giant" and "The Canterville Ghost" warrant special
mention. He wrote only one novel, *The Picture of Dorian
Gray*, which is one of the finest written during a literary
golden age that G. K. Chesterton celebrated in his *Victorian Age in Literature*.

It is, however, ironic that Wilde is not remembered
by most people for his literary *oeuvre* but for the scandal
surrounding his private life. Having deserted his wife and
two young sons in pursuit of the homosexual lifestyle, he
was sent to prison in 1895. Demonized by his contemporaries for the moral iconoclasm of his sexual choices,
he is now lionized by many as a "martyr" for the cause
of homosexual "liberation". The risibly inappropriate
nature of the latter judgment is made manifest by Wilde's
description of his own homosexuality as a "pathology", a
statement that could land him in gaol in some European
countries in our own "liberated" age for the heinous crime
of "homophobia".

Wilde died in disgraced exile, in Paris, in garret poverty, fearing that future generations would see only the

marsh water of his murky "loves", leaving the wine of his art untasted. In his final hours, he was received into the Catholic Church, being fortified and consoled by the Last Rites. It was the consummation of a lifelong and flirtatious love affair with Christ and His Church that stretched back to his days as an undergraduate in Dublin.

What are we to make of this most beguiled and beguiling, this most confused and confusing of men? Does he have anything of value to teach us? Is his work of relevance to our own times?

As we set about trying to answer these questions, we are confronted and perhaps affronted by the provocative Preface with which Wilde raises the curtain on his novel. It says something of the power of Wilde's aphoristic wit, which was the toast of the salons of London and Paris prior to his downfall, that the two-page Preface is almost as well known as the novel itself and that it almost outshines it in brilliance. Take, for example, Wilde's vituperatively splenetic judgment on his own age:

> *The nineteenth century dislike of realism is the rage of Caliban seeing his own face in a glass.*

> *The nineteenth century dislike of romanticism is the rage of Caliban not seeing his own face in a glass.*[1]

For Wilde, late Victorian England is synonymous with the monstrous subhuman character in Shakespeare's *The Tempest* who is bereft of all culture, all civilized values, and all Christian virtues, whose physical deformity is a reflection of his moral and spiritual ugliness, and whose very

---

[1] Oscar Wilde, *The Picture of Dorian Gray*, ed. Joseph Pearce, Ignatius Critical Editions (San Francisco: Ignatius Press, 2008), 3 (italics in original here and below).

name, effectively an anagram of *cannibal*, cries out against him. Such an age hates realism because it cannot bear to see the ugly truth about itself, but it also hates romanticism because it refuses to see the existence of a beauty beyond its own ugliness. An age that can't bear to look at itself and can't bear to look beyond itself is in trouble!

Having held up a Swiftian mirror of satirical scorn to his own age, revealing its ugliness, he praises those who are open to the gifts of beauty.

> *Those who find ugly meanings in beautiful things are corrupt without being charming. This is a fault.*
>
> *Those who find beautiful meanings in beautiful things are the cultivated. For these there is hope.*[2]

This emphatically nonrelativistic emphasis on the objective presence of beauty, which is not in the eye of the beholder but is present in spite of the beholder's ability to see it, serves as a condemnation of the blindness of cynicism that cannot see beauty, perceiving only ugliness. One is reminded of a line from one of Wilde's plays in which a cynic is defined as one who knows the price of everything and the value of nothing. The cynic is a relativist who cannot see that which is intrinsically beautiful, a thing's inherent value, but only that which is subject to the fluctuations of his own fleeting feelings, the price that he assigns to it at any given time and that is always subject to change.

Thus far, Wilde is revealing himself in the Preface to his novel as a tradition-oriented aesthete, reflecting his long-standing preference for the traditionalist aesthetic of John Ruskin over that of the modernist Walter Pater, both of whom had influenced Wilde deeply in his formative

[2] Ibid.

years at Oxford. The problem is that this traditionalist aesthetic is largely ignored by modern critics who prefer to accentuate Wilde's claim in the same Preface that art is beyond morality.

> There is no such thing as a moral or an immoral book. Books are well written, or badly written. That is all.[3]

This elevation of beauty over morality does violence to the traditional transcendental synthesis of the good, the true, and the beautiful, which Christian philosophers have rightly connected to the Trinity itself. To separate the beautiful from the good (virtue) and the true (reason) is to do violence to the cosmos itself. To split the trinity of the transcendentals is the ontological equivalent of splitting the atom, as explosive and as destructive metaphysically as the atom bomb is physically. It is no wonder that Wilde's iconoclastic bomb, dropped with seeming nonchalance into the midst of his Preface, is quoted *ad nauseam* by those seeking the nihilistic destruction and deconstruction of meaning itself.

There is, however, a delicious irony in the fact that Wilde flagrantly denies and defies his own aphorism in the writing of the novel, in which he presents in the denouement of the plot a vision of morality that is profoundly Christian and that seems to prophesy his own eventual conversion. In essence, following the Faustian tradition, Wilde tells the story of a man (Dorian Gray) who, inspired by his own vanity and by the iconoclastic philosophy of his satanic tempter (Lord Henry Wotton), sells his soul to the devil in return for the retention of his boyish good looks. As Gray indulges his sensual appetites with an increasingly

[3] Ibid.

insatiable hunger, his portrait grows uglier and more cruel, a mirror of the corruption of his soul.

In the midst of Gray's descent into ever-deepening pits of depravity, he is given a "yellow book" by Lord Henry Wotton, which, from the description that Wilde gives of its lurid plot, is quite obviously Huysmans' decadent masterpiece, À Rebours, a novel that depicts the protagonist's life of sheer sensual self-indulgence—leading, via ennui, to an ultimate scream of despair and a desperate desire for God. Wilde's protagonist follows the same downward path, except that Dorian Gray refuses to repent. Instead, he begins to despise the portrait, which is now hideously grotesque and spattered with the blood that he had spilled. Seeing the painting as a reflection of his conscience and indeed as a reflection of his soul, he decides to destroy it so that he might enjoy his sins without the painting's hideous reminder of their consequences. His effort to destroy it proves fatal, indeed suicidal. The moral, as inescapable as it is clear, is that the killing of the conscience is the killing of the soul and that the killing of the soul is the killing of the self.

In his own appraisal of the novel, Wilde contradicted his own aphorism by stating that "there is a terrible moral in Dorian Gray—a moral which the prurient will not be able to find in it, but which will be revealed to all whose minds are healthy."[4] Like all good art, of which the portrait of Dorian Gray is itself a powerful symbol, Wilde's novel holds up a mirror to its reader. It shows us ourselves and teaches us the terrible lessons that we need to learn.

There are indeed such things as moral and immoral books, whether well written or badly written. Moral books show us ourselves and our place in the cosmos. They are

---

[4] St. James Gazette, June 26, 1890.

152 CLASSIC LITERATURE MADE SIMPLE

epiphanies of grace. Immoral books are like Lord Henry Wotton in Wilde's story or indeed like the devil himself in the story in which we are all living. They are liars and deceivers who show us a false picture of ourselves and the world in which we live. Moral books wake us up; immoral books lull us to sleep. *The Picture of Dorian Gray* wakes us up, stirring us from the somnambulant path of least resistance that leads to hell. It is for this reason, if for no other, that we should thank heaven for the vision of hell that Wilde's novel reveals to us.

33

The Path to Rome

The Path to Rome is arguably the finest work of literature that Hilaire Belloc ever wrote. This, apparently, was the view of Belloc himself, as expressed in an inscription in his own personal copy of the book, written six years after its first publication in 1902, that "Alas! I never shall so write again!" It seems that he never altered this judgment irrespective of the numerous volumes he would write in the following decades. Writing to an American friend, Carl Schmidt, in 1930, he declared that his novel *Belinda* was "certainly the book of mine which I like best since I wrote *The Path to Rome*".[1] It is clear, therefore, that the best of Belloc is to be found on the path to Rome.

On the literal level, *The Path to Rome* is simply and ostensibly a factual account of the author's pilgrimage in 1901. Setting off on foot from Toul, in France, Belloc travels through the valley of the Moselle, heading for Switzerland and then, traversing the Alps, to Italy. Traveling with him, mile by mile and page by page, as he trudges the 750 miles to the Eternal City, the reader sees Europe at the turn of a new century, over a century ago, through the eyes of a

---

[1] Hilaire Belloc to Carl Schmidt, May 16, 1930, Special Collection, O'Shaugnessy-Frey Library, Minnesota; quoted in Joseph Pearce, *Old Thunder: A Life of Hilaire Belloc* (London: Harper Collins, 2002), 234.

poet besotted with its beauty. We see it through the lens of a historian who understands the living majesty of Europe's past. We see it through the faithful heart of a Catholic who beholds a vision of the Europe of the faith in which the present is seen to be in vivid and vibrant communion with the past. This would be enough in itself to warrant our reading of the book. After all, who would not want to step back in time to follow the indefatigable Belloc, step by step, on a pilgrimage through Europe, with Belloc himself as the guide? One is tempted, indeed, to see this as a pilgrimage made in heaven.

In terms of its formal structure and literary genre, *The Path to Rome* is both a travelogue and a farrago, which is to say that it is, at one and the same time, a linear narrative connected to a journey, and a seemingly random dispersal of anecdotal thoughts and musings. It is animated, therefore, by the tension between the forward momentum maintained by the author's account of his pilgrimage and the inertial force of the tangential interruptions and digressions. Whereas the literal linear narrative represents the horizontal dimension of the work, the digressionary musings signify the vertical movement of the contemplating soul toward the things of God. This combination constitutes a distinct literary genre, and one in which Belloc excelled. Having experimented with what might be called the "travel-farrago" in the writing of *The Path to Rome*, he would return to it with great success in *The Four Men* and *The Cruise of the "Nona"*.

This understanding of the book's formal and structural dimension does not do justice to the metaphorical and metaphysical dimensions, which transform *The Path to Rome* into a work of mystery and mysticism, in which Belloc, like Dante in *The Divine Comedy*, is transfigured into Everyman, an image and figure of all of us on our respective pilgrimages through life. He makes and breaks vows, learning priceless lessons in the process; he loses precious possessions that he might no longer be possessed by them; he discovers an oasis in what he thought would be nothing but a desert; he suffers humiliation in order to attain humility; his pride is broken that he might be healed; the blisters on his feet become the cross he must carry. He is a much smaller man at the end of the journey than he thought he was at its beginning, and he is much closer to heaven in consequence.

Belloc, as the archetypal pilgrim, is *homo viator*, whose journey toward the Eternal City of Rome is symbolic of the journey of each of us toward the Eternal City of God. In this sense, the journey becomes a metaphor for life itself, indicative of the providential connection between the experience of life and its deeper meaning, the quest for Rome becoming the quest for heaven. As J. R. R. Tolkien once remarked, life is a study for eternity for those so gifted. It is no wonder, therefore, that *The Path to Rome* is a work of humility and awe, of gratitude and hope, of faith and love. But, like us, it is also carnal. It is incarnational. It is flesh, mystically communing with, and exiled from, heaven, but also rooted in the earth. It is pithy and earthy, anecdotal and tangential; it is simultaneously prayerfully reverent and playfully irreverent. It is a faith loved and lived within the constraints of the fallible and fallen nature of the author. And as for the author's motivation for writing the book, Belloc inscribed in his own personal copy that "I wrote this book for the glory of God."

From the pregnant poignancy of Belloc's superb preface, with its delightful combination of the wistful and the whimsical, to the dash and dare of the wonderful poem that serves as the book's, and the pilgrim's, conclusion, *The Path to Rome* takes the reader on a journey into himself and out of himself, a voyage of discovery in which home and exile are interwoven in a mystical dance of contemplation. In its pages, we discover the Europe of the faith, which was, and is, the heart of Christendom, and the faith itself, which was, and is, the heart of all.

34

The Four Men

Hilaire Belloc wrote on literally anything and everything, "literally" being meant quite literally. His book *On Anything*, published in 1910, had been preceded the previous year by his book *On Everything*. He also published *On Nothing* in 1908 and *On Something* in 1910. Then, in 1923, he took the omnivorous whimsy to its utmost conclusion, publishing *On*. Such volumes display Belloc's versatility as an essayist, illustrating not only the many facets of his Catholicism but also his catholicity of taste for anything, for everything and, most beguilingly, for nothing in particular. Thus, for instance, he writes "On the Pleasure of Taking Up One's Pen", "On Ignorance", "On Tea", "On Them", "On Death", "On Experience", "On Sacramental Things", "On Song", "On the Rights of Property", "On Old Towns" and, appropriately enough at the conclusion of one of the volumes, "On Coming to an End". In the pages of these meandering miscellanies one discovers more about Belloc the man than is discernible in any of his other works except for those hauntingly personal pilgrimages of the soul, *The Path to Rome* (1902), *The Four Men* (1912), and *The Cruise of the "Nona"* (1925), in which the author waxes wistful and whimsical on the first things, the permanent things, and in general on the things (and the Thing) that give meaning to, and make sense of, anything and everything else.

These three "pilgrimages", taken together, might be dubbed "travel-farragoes", a distinct literary genre in which Belloc excelled. As discussed in the previous "nutshell" on *The Path to Rome*, they are, at one and the same time, both travelogues and farragoes—linear narratives connected to a journey interspersed with seemingly random anecdotal musings on anything and everything. As such, they are not for those who are in a hurry but for those who wish to saunter with the author in the leisurely pursuit of those things that are worth pursuing at leisure; and those things worth pursuing at leisure are, of course, the very things that are worth spending our whole lives getting to know better.

Although *The Path to Rome* was, according to Belloc's own appraisal, the best book he ever wrote, there is little doubt that *The Four Men* warrants a place of distinction as one of the finest works of this finest of writers. Although it was not published until 1912, Belloc seems to have embarked on it as early as 1907, originally planning to call it *The County of Sussex*. In 1909 he told Maurice Baring that it would describe "myself and three other characters walking through the county; the other characters are really supernatural beings, a poet, a sailor and Grizzlebeard.... They only turn out to be supernatural beings when we get to the town of Liss, which is just over the Hampshire border."[1]

Although the "four men" are figments of Belloc's imagination, they are also facets of his own character. Belloc was himself a poet and a sailor, whereas the elderly character Grizzlebeard could be seen as those aspects of Belloc's character which were rooted in the past: Belloc the historian, the Catholic, and the traditionalist. As for the fourth man,

[1] Hilaire Belloc to Maurice Baring, December 4, 1909, quoted in Robert Speaight, *The Life of Hilaire Belloc* (New York: Books for Libraries Press, 1970), 325.

Myself, he is the narrative voice that holds the whole thing together. As they walk the length of the county of Sussex, these four characters discourse on this, that, and just about everything else: on local eccentrics and local saints; on "awful towns" ruined by modernity that need to be avoided like the plague; on the worst and best things in the world; on fairies; on the holy sacrifice of the Mass; on the money devil; on the singing of kettles and the singing of drinking songs; on the birth of rivers, the hammering of heretics, and the curing of pigs; on inns; on the soul; on worried ghosts and the dead who haunt the dreams of men; on the very best beer; on ancient kings and legendary wars; on hunting men and horses; on first loves and noble sacrifices; on strange philosophers and singing dukes; on politicians who sell their souls; on eggs and bacon and cheese; on the breaking of bread and the breaking of fellowship.

The Path to Rome and *The Four Men* are pilgrimages conveying a soul's love for the soil of its native land, which in the former case is the macrocosmic "Europe of the Faith" in which Belloc was raised, and in the latter case is the microcosmic Shire in which he was also raised. Home, like Rome, is a "holy place", and *The Four Men* is full of spiritual premonitions of "the character of enduring things" amid the decay of time:

> It has been proved in the life of every man that though his loves are human, and therefore changeable, yet in proportion as he attaches them to things unchangeable, so they mature and broaden.
>
> On this account ... does a man love an old house, which was his father's, and on this account does a man come to love with all his heart, that part of earth which nourished his boyhood.[2]

---

[2] Hilaire Belloc, preface to *The Four Men* (London: Thomas Nelson, 1948), v.

One is struck upon reading these wistfully eloquent words from the preface to *The Four Men* with their similarity to the preface to *The Path to Rome*, in which Belloc had written that "one's native place is the shell of one's soul, and one's church is the kernel of that nut."[3] In both books, he lays the foundations of what might be termed the "theology of place". This concept, which can be said to be truly at the heart of Belloc's work, is quintessentially incarnational. A sense of "place" is linked to the love of home, and the love of home is itself salted by the home's temporary absence or unattainability. Paradoxically, it is the sense of exile that gives the love of home its intensity and its power. The theology of place is therefore rooted in the earth and yet reaches to heaven. It is expressed most sublimely in the *Salve Regina*, in which the "poor banished children of Eve", lost in "this vale of tears", hope that, "after this our exile", we might behold the Blessed Fruit of our Mother's womb, Jesus, who is the soul's true home.

This understanding of the spiritual significance of "home", this theology of place, is such a recurrent theme in Belloc's work that it could be said to be almost omnipresent. Few writers have felt so intensely the sense of exile, and hence the love of home, to the degree to which it is invoked by Belloc. From the love of Sussex at the heart of *The Four Men* and in poems such as "Ha'nacker Mill" or "The South Country", to the love of Europe in general, and France in particular, evoked in *The Path to Rome* and in poems such as "Tarantella", his work resonates with the love of earth as a foreshadowing of the love of heaven. It is in this soil-soul nexus that the nub of Belloc's profundity is to be discovered. It manifests itself in the tension between permanence and mutability, and finds infectious expression in the perfect balance between wistfulness and whimsy. Although these qualities are to be found in all of Belloc's work, as expressions of the very spirit of the man himself, they are to be found to an exceptional degree in *The Path to Rome* and *The Four Men*.

In my introduction to the Ignatius Press edition of *The Path to Rome*, I wrote that "*The Four Men* rivals it, and perhaps surpasses it, as a vehicle for Belloc's wit and wisdom, or as an outpouring of his irrepressible personality."[4] Since Belloc considered *The Path to Rome* his best work, it seems that I am in disagreement with the great man himself in such effusive praise of *The Four Men*. No matter. Even if we are to defer to Belloc's own judgment, it is no small thing to be Belloc's second best, or even his third best book. In any event, like all of Belloc's books, it deserves to be read and reread by all who hunger for the "enduring things" in an age of deplorable change.

[4] Ibid., vii.

35

By What Authority?

Robert Hugh Benson's reception into the Catholic Church in 1903 was the most seismic of all the conversions of the Catholic Cultural Revival, with the sole exception of John Henry Newman's. The fact that Benson was the son of the Archbishop of Canterbury, the Anglican "pope" (so to speak), sent shockwaves through the establishment in general and the established church in particular. It represented further proof that Catholicism was emerging as a potent religious and cultural force in contemporary England and that the faith could no longer be dismissed or marginalized. It was confirmation that the Catholic Church had "arrived"—or, more correctly, that she had returned!

Benson's autobiographical *Confessions of a Convert*, in which he charted the course by which he had found his way from Canterbury to Rome, is a real classic of conversion literature. Apart from Augustine's incomparable *Confessions* and Newman's *Apologia*, there are few more powerful testimonies of a soul's journey to Rome than Benson's own *Confessions*.

A later prominent convert, who was hugely influenced by Benson and is often mentioned in association with him, is Ronald Knox. The son of the Bishop of Manchester, Knox was received into the Church in 1917, three years after Benson's tragic and untimely death. In the last few days before his reception, Knox had read several Catholic novels, enjoying Benson's *Come Rack! Come Rope!* the most: "Hugh Benson, who had set my feet on the way towards the Church, watched over my footsteps to the last."[1]

Come Rack! Come Rope! is set in Elizabethan England, as is *By What Authority?* In both novels, the period of the English Reformation is brought to blood-curdling life. The reader, if he allows himself to be carried thither, will find himself transported to the late sixteenth century, the terror and tension of the times gripping him as tightly as it grips the leading characters, who gave courageous witness to their faith in a hostile and deadly environment.

Benson seems to have written much of *By What Authority?* before his reception into the Church in September 1903. According to Dom Bede Camm, who spent time with Benson in the days immediately after the latter's conversion, Benson was keen to learn as much as possible about the Elizabethan period:

> He ... began to consult me on the book he was writing on the Elizabethan persecution.... He poured out the details of the book, as it was shaping itself, and eagerly seized on any points that would be of use to him. In the end it was settled that I should read and correct the proof-sheets and do my best to help him secure historical accuracy.[2]

It was a year later, in October 1904, after a period in which Benson fretted about whether he would be able to find a publisher for his first Catholic book, that Dom Bede Camm finally finished reading the proofs. Having done so,

[1] Ronald Knox, *A Spiritual Aeneid* (London: Burns Oates, 1958), 215.
[2] C. C. Martindale, S.J., *The Life of Monsignor Robert Hugh Benson*, vol. 1 (London: Longmans, Green and Co., 1916), 266.

he persuaded Benson to change the title of the novel from *Magnus Valde* to the more accessible and comprehensible *By What Authority?*

Benson was wise and prudent to enlist the services of a Catholic historian of Dom Bede's stature to help him iron out the historical creases. It was, therefore, little wonder that he should write in the frontispiece to the novel of his "wish to acknowledge a great debt of gratitude to the Reverend Dom Bede Camm, O.S.B., who kindly read this book in proof, and made many valuable suggestions".

As for the novel itself, it brings the period of the Tudor terror to life in a way that is hardly possible in a nonfictional historical narrative. We get to know the characters as they come to terms with the tyrannous time in which they're living. There is the suffering of the recusant Catholics, the courage and sanctity of some and the apostasy of others, and the heroism of Protestant converts to the faith. We are taken into the very presence of Bloody Bess herself, the cold queen, as Chesterton dubbed her, whose narcissism and cruelty is chillingly depicted. Last and indubitably least are those traitors and turncoats, whose treachery betrayed Catholics to their deaths.

The most perceptive observation of *By What Authority?* was made by Benson's biographer, C. C. Martindale, who observed that "Benson really teaches that, as in the *Aeneid* it is Rome, not Aeneas, who is 'hero' and gives the piece its unity."[3] Father Martindale's point is that Christ, in His Mystical Body, the Church, is the real hero of the novel. Just as Virgil's purpose was to eulogize Rome, not Aeneas, so Benson's purpose was to eulogize Rome, not any of the individual characters of the novel, even those who exhibit the most heroism in the service of Rome. The beauty of

[3] Ibid., 364.

By What Authority? is nothing less than the beauty of the Church made manifest in its pages. "The supreme factor is a City", Father Martindale writes; "or, if you will, that the two cities which Augustine saw, eternally opposed, God's and the world's, were here and now incarnated in Rome and England."[4] If one were to beg to differ with this sagacious reading of the novel, it would be only to insist that the English Martyrs were as English as Elizabeth I. It is they and not she who are the jewel in England's crown. The England for which they died is the Catholic England, the Merrie England, which Elizabeth and her bloody servants were seeking to kill. This true England was also being martyred in the martyrdom of her holy sons and daughters. This true England is worth celebrating as is this novel which brings such an England to vibrant and vigorous life.

[4] Ibid.

36

Lord of the World

Robert Hugh Benson is best known for historical fiction. In novels such as *The King's Achievement, By What Authority?*, and *Come Rack! Come Rope!*, he takes the reader into the dark and deadly heart of the Tudor terror during the reigns of Henry VIII and Elizabeth I in the sixteenth century. In *Richard Raynal, Solitary*, the reader is taken a century further back in time to the happier, merrier England of the early fifteenth century to meet the colorful character of "Master Richard", a holy hermit on a God-given mission. Such was Benson's genius, however, that he was not constrained by any one literary genre. Aside from his historical romances, he was equally adept at novels with a contemporary setting, such as *The Necromancers*, a cautionary tale about the dangers of spiritualism, or with dystopic futuristic fantasies, such as *Lord of the World*, which warrants a place beside Aldous Huxley's *Brave New World* and George Orwell's *Nineteen Eighty-Four* as a classic of dystopian fiction and as a work of prophecy. Each of these cautionary tales set in an imaginary future has a prophetic element that remains as relevant as ever. Huxley warns of the corrupting influence of the pursuit of comfort, showing a society that somnambulates toward luxurious slavery; Orwell shows the sheer horror of totalitarian control over the lives of individuals; Benson shows how atheism, in the guise of secular humanism, emerges as a rival religion to Christianity, intent on global domination.

The principal characters of *Lord of the World* are realistically and sympathetically depicted, even those who advocate the new atheism. Such a balanced and genuinely humane approach to the dignity of the human person is a characteristic of all of Benson's novels. He never falls into the trap of reducing his characters to two-dimensional caricatures. There are no devilishly wicked or psychopathic villains, and there are no angelic sin-free, sugar-coated saints. Such realism saves his work from the preachiness that is the death of so much Christian fiction. (Indeed, Benson's work should be studied diligently by all those who wish to write Christian fiction well.)

The two priests at the center of *Lord of the World* are Father Percy Franklin and Father John Francis. The former is devout, though troubled with doubt; the latter is an apostate who becomes a high-profile practitioner of the new secular humanist "religion". The other primary characters are Oliver and Mabel Brand, a socialist politician and his wife. They are both likable, insofar as they are genuinely idealistic and fully believe in the creed of secular humanism, and insofar as they genuinely love each other as husband and wife, each desiring the good of the other. Such is Benson's skill and finesse as a storyteller that we almost believe that the new "progressive" humanism can really be beneficial to humanity, replacing the antiquated "other-worldly" religions of the world with practical plans for changing this world for the better. It all seems so plausible, especially when advocated by Julian Felsenburgh, the elusive yet pervasive "Lord of the World" himself, who travels the globe preaching peace. Such are his charismatic and rhetorical gifts that he does not merely preach peace

168   CLASSIC LITERATURE MADE SIMPLE

but he makes peace, persuading the global superpowers to pull back from the brink of impending war.

Felsenburgh's political and diplomatic success, bringing harmony in the name of humanity, make him a global celebrity whose name is on everyone's lips. Devotion to his personality and the policies he advocates takes on a pseudo-religious fervor. He soon becomes the most powerful force in world politics. National governments prostrate themselves at his feet, giving him absolute control of world affairs. The only global opposition to this globalist dominion is to be found in the Catholic Church, the other Christian denominations having been seduced by modernism and subsumed within the secularist spirit of the age. The non-Christian religions have succumbed to Felsenburgh's charms and have reached an accommodation with his plans for the world.

As the true spirit of the Lord of the World becomes clear in the increasingly brutal persecution of the Church, the fortitude of the heroic Father Franklin is tested to the limit, as is the idealism of Oliver and Mabel Brand, which is put to the test in its encounter with the inhumane policies of Felsenburgh's humanitarian regime.

Considering that *Lord of the World* was published in 1907, twenty-five years before the publication of Huxley's novel and forty-two years earlier than Orwell's *Nineteen Eighty-Four*, it can claim preeminence in terms of its prophetic power. Huxley and Orwell were both writing after the Bolshevik Revolution and Mussolini's March on Rome and were able to see the consequences of communist and fascist totalitarianism with the wisdom of hindsight. Benson, on the other hand, was writing ten years before the Russian Revolution and fifteen years before the rise of fascism in Italy. *Lord of the World* actually predicts a revolution in 1917, though it occurs in Britain, not in

Russia, and results in a one-party totalitarian socialist state. The novel also foresees the use of flying machines to bomb civilian populations in cities, thirty years before the Nazi and fascist bombing of Guernica during the Spanish Civil War and the so-called blitzkrieg unleashed on the cities of England in 1940. The novel even appears to predict the dropping of bombs that are so powerful that whole cities can be wiped out, prefiguring the dropping of the atomic bombs on Hiroshima and Nagasaki.

Lord of the World also foresees with astonishing prescience the rise of the cult of personality, incarnated in the novel by the idolization of Julian Felsenburgh, long before the rise of Lenin, Stalin, Mussolini, and Hitler. When Orwell presents us with Big Brother in the late 1940s, he reminds us of totalitarian tyrants who had already disgraced and disfigured history; Benson's "Lord of the World" is ahead of his time and is much more subtle, believable, and likable than Orwell's brutalist "Big Brother", as well as being ultimately demonic and not merely monstrous and therefore much creepier. Above all, Benson's classic of dystopian fiction foresees and foreshadows the rise of globalism and the secular humanist atheism as a new godless religion. His cautionary vision of the future is becoming the present in which we find ourselves.

The world depicted in *Lord of the World* is one where creeping secularism and godless humanism have triumphed over traditional morality. It is a world where philosophical relativism has triumphed over objectivity; a world where, in the name of tolerance, religious doctrine is not tolerated. It is a world where euthanasia is practiced widely and religion hardly practiced at all. The lord of this nightmare world is a benign-looking politician intent on power in the name of "peace", and intent on the destruction of religion in the name of "truth". In such a world, only a small and shrinking Church stands resolutely against the demonic "Lord of the World".

As for the novel's perennial relevance, it was evident in 1992 when Cardinal Ratzinger (the future Pope Benedict XVI) cited it as a means of criticizing a recent speech in which President George H. W. Bush had called for "a New World Order". During his 1992 talk at Milan's Catholic University, the future pope sought to remind the U.S. president that Benson's novel had already described a similar "unified civilization and its power to destroy the spirit. The anti-Christ is represented as the great carrier of peace in a similar new world order." Cardinal Ratzinger then quoted from Pope Benedict XV's 1920 encyclical *Bonum sane*: "The coming of a world state is longed for, by all the worst and most distorted elements. This state, based on the principles of absolute equality of men and a community of possessions, would banish all national loyalties. In it no acknowledgement would be made of the authority of a father over his children, or of God over human society. If these ideas are put into practice, there will inevitably follow a reign of unheard-of terror."[1] Such a state is foreseen in *Lord of the World*, which is why it should be on the reading list of all lovers of authentic human freedom.

[1] Quoted by Monsignor Luigi Negri in his comments on *The Lord of the World* in "'Ideological Colonization' in *Lord of the World*", *Inside the Vatican* (magazine), March 1, 2015, https://insidethevatican.com/magazine/culture/ideological-colonization-in-lord-of-the-world/.

37

The Man Who Was Thursday

Considering that G. K. Chesterton is the master of paradox, we should not be surprised to discover that his greatest novel is itself the greatest of paradoxes. *The Man Who Was Thursday* is the darkest and lightest of novels, as well as being one of the most beguiling and confusing. Subtitled *A Nightmare*, it is a dark and dismal dreamscape, predating and perhaps prophesying the rise of surrealism, though very different from surrealism in its inspirational source and in its solution to the problems posed by the psychological subjectivism that it confronts.

The novel's inspirational source was Chesterton's own experience of the decadence of the 1890s and his recoiling in horror from the radical pessimism of fashionable philosophers, such as Schopenhauer. Speaking in old age of his experience of such subjectivism as an impressionable young man, he wrote that "my eyes were turned inwards rather than outwards; giving my moral personality, I should imagine, a very unattractive squint."[1] He was

> still oppressed with the metaphysical nightmare of negations about mind and matter, with the morbid imagery of evil, with the burden of my own mysterious brain and

[1] G. K. Chesterton, *Autobiography* (New York: Sheed & Ward, 1936), 97.

body; but by this time I was in revolt against them; and trying to construct a healthier conception of cosmic life, even if it were one that should err on the side of health. I even called myself an optimist, because I was so horribly near to being a pessimist. It is the only excuse I can offer.[2]

These lines from Chesterton's autobiography immediately precede his discussion of *The Man Who Was Thursday*, indicating that the novel grew from the murkiness and mawkishness of the author's doubt-filled adolescence: "The whole story is a nightmare of things, not as they are, but as they seemed to the young half-pessimist of the '90s."[3]

Although *The Man Who Was Thursday* is *inspired* by the confusion of the *fin de siècle*, it *aspires* to dispel and disperse the clouds of despondency with the piercing light of Christian clarity and charity. It cannot be stressed enough that this critical distance between the *inspirational* and *aspirational* aspects of the novel is crucial to our understanding of it. *Thursday* was written at around the same time that Chesterton was also writing *Orthodoxy*, his masterpiece of Christian apologetics, both books being published in 1908, and it is perilous to our understanding of the former book if we fail to read it in the light of the latter.

Seeing *Thursday* in the contemporaneous light of *Orthodoxy* and its "ethics of elfland", we can see that it encapsulates the paradox, embodied in the character of Chesterton's delightful priest-detective Father Brown, that wisdom can be found only in innocence. This is nothing less than the truth that Christ teaches. We will not be with Him in heaven unless we become as little children.

[2] Ibid., 97–98.
[3] Ibid., 98.

The paradoxical heart of *The Man Who Was Thursday* is the tension that exists between the *childlikeness* demanded by Christ and the *childishness* that St. Paul tells us to avoid. We have to remain *childlike* by ceasing to be *childish*. The first is the wisdom of innocence, or the sanity of sanctity, whereby we see the miracle of life with eyes full of wonder; the second is the self-centeredness of one who refuses the challenge of growing up. Chesterton's *Man Who Was Thursday* is essentially about childish detectives attaining childlike wisdom, just as his later novel, *Manalive*, illustrates how the pure childlikeness of the aptly named Innocent Smith is misunderstood by the childish world in which he finds himself.

These priceless lessons are taught in *The Man Who Was Thursday* through the quest for truth of six philosopher-detectives and their efforts to uncover the real identity of the mysterious character of Sunday, the president of the Central Anarchist Council. These detectives infiltrate the anarchist council on the orders of a chief of police who is as mysterious as Sunday himself.

As the "six philosophers" unmask each other, one by one, each having suspected that the others were anarchists, they realize that Sunday has tricked them and has played a joke on them for no discernible reason. All that is then left is the quest to unmask Sunday. As the chase begins, Chesterton, as a master of the detective story, provides priceless clues, which are so well concealed that the reader misses them, as do the detectives. He gives three clues in quick succession to the identity of Sunday, which connects him to the divine attributes of omnipotence, omnipresence, and omniscience. These go unnoticed as we pursue more obvious clues that are finally revealed as red herrings. Chesterton leads the reader on a wild goose chase in the quest for Sunday, in much the same way as Sunday himself leads the detectives on such a chase. The meaning of the quest is finally revealed as the adventure of true philosophy to remove the secret "mask" that is worn by a peaceful, suffering, and ultimately mirthful God. This ultimate purpose and goal of philosophy is revealed at the novel's climax. Indeed, like all good detective stories, the mystery is solved in the final pages. Or is it? It is the mark of the beguiling brilliance of *The Man Who Was Thursday* that many or most readers are still scratching their heads even after the final mask is removed.

The ending of the novel is, however, less complicated than we might think it is. Sunday refers to himself within the context of the Book of Genesis and the days of Creation as "the Sabbath" and "the peace of God",[4] and, as if to hammer the point home, his final words are those of Christ Himself, asking his interlocutors, "Can ye drink of the cup that I drink of?"[5] We simply need to take Sunday at his word. He is the peace of God and, at the same time, he is the suffering God. The ending of the novel should be read in parallel with the ending of *Orthodoxy*, which was written at around the same time. *Orthodoxy* ends with the suggestion that God plays hide-and-seek and that the one thing that he is always hiding is his mirth. This should also be seen in the light of Chesterton's poem "The Skeleton", in which death is described as the good king's jest. It is this God of peace and mirth whose presence makes sense of the real suffering and nonsensical nightmare that His perceived absence presents.

The Man Who Was Thursday shows us the paradoxical truth that it takes a big man to know how small he is. It

---

[4] G. K. Chesterton, *The Man Who Was Thursday*, in vol. 6 of *The Collected Works of G. K. Chesterton*, comp. Denis J. Conlon (San Francisco: Ignatius Press, 1991), 631.
[5] Ibid., 634.

shows us that thinking we are big is childish while knowing that we are small is childlike. Thinking we are big, the sin of pride, turns our world into a living nightmare. Knowing we are small wakes us up. In a world that is somnambulating deeper and deeper into the living nightmare it has made for itself, we are in more need than ever of the wide-awake awareness of G. K. Chesterton, a visionary who was larger than life because he spent his life on his knees.

38

The Ball and the Cross

Although *The Man Who Was Thursday* is probably the best and certainly the best-known of Chesterton's novels, it is not by any means the only novel of his which is worthy of merit and therefore worth mentioning. *The Napoleon of Notting Hill* is a futuristic political novel advocating small government and localism, which was dedicated to the great localist Hilaire Belloc and was admired by the great enemy of big government, George Orwell. *The Flying Inn* is a rambunctious romp in defense of merriment and in defiance of puritanism, which celebrates good things such as ale and cheese, and censures bad things such as Islam and Prohibition. *Manalive* is a parable on the difference between childlike wisdom and childish wickedness in which the aptly named protagonist Innocent Smith is so misunderstood that he is presumed guilty until proven innocent. And yet, of all Chesterton's novels, with the exception of *The Man Who Was Thursday*, the one most worth reading is probably *The Ball and the Cross*.

First published in serial form in the pages of the British journal *The Commonwealth* in 1905 and 1906, *The Ball and the Cross* was first published in book form in the United States in 1909 and in the United Kingdom a year later. Its overarching spirit can be encapsulated in a comment that Chesterton made of his relationship with his brother, Cecil. They were always arguing, said Chesterton, but

never quarreled. The whole novel is delightfully argumen-
tative, in the sense that there is not a protagonist and an
antagonist but only two antagonists, MacIan and Turnbull,
a Catholic and an atheist, respectively, who are intent on
fighting a duel in defense of their beliefs.

As we get to know them and as they get to know each
other, we see how they come to respect and ultimately
even to like each other, in spite of their fundamental differences. As with the six detectives in *The Man Who Was
Thursday*, we come to realize that the authentic quest for
truth, rooted in the goodness and beauty of reason, is a
noble endeavor. The real villains are not MacIan and Turnbull, who both believe in the objectivity of reality, but the
various types of relativists whom they meet, none of whom
believe in truth and none of whom, in consequence, feel
that truth is worth fighting for and still less dying for.

With the proto-surrealism that would also characterize *The
Man Who Was Thursday*, the novel is framed within a weird,
dreamlike first and final chapter indicative of the supernatural
setting of all reality. The novel begins in a flying ship with
two characters, Professor Lucifer, the mad and demonic sci-
entist who had invented the ship, and a holy monk called
Michael. Parallels with *The Man Who Was Thursday*, which
begins with an argument between characters named Lucien
and Gabriel, are inescapable. At the foundation of everything
is the primal struggle between light and darkness, between
good and evil, between God and Satan. Whether Professor Lucifer is the devil himself, he is certainly of the devil's
party; and even though the holy monk, Michael, might not
be his archangelic namesake, he is certainly on the side of
the angels. The whole action of the novel is set, therefore,
within a theological cosmological framework.

The novel gets its title from the ball and the cross that
surmount the dome of St. Paul's Cathedral in London. This

invites yet another parallel with *The Man Who Was Thursday* in which Gabriel Syme is inspired by "the great orb and the cross"[1] of St. Paul's to raise his sword-stick in salute to the symbolism it represents: "It seemed a symbol of human faith and valour."[2] On a deeper symbolic level, it could be said that the ball and the cross also represent the City of Man and the City of God. It does so in two distinct ways. First, Turnbull's atheism represents the reduction of reality to mere matter (the ball), whereas MacIan's Catholicism represents the dilation of reality into the presence of the divine as revealed in the life, death, and Resurrection of Christ (the cross). Second, however, it represents the secularized relativism of most of the characters of the novel who seek nothing but their own self-gratification and comfort (the ball signifying the City of Man), whereas Turnbull and MacIan are willing to sacrifice themselves in pursuit of that objective truth, which is ultimately God Himself. They are crusaders, even though Turnbull doesn't know it, who take up their swords in defense of the truth. In taking up their swords, in their willingness to suffer for the sake of truth, they are simultaneously taking up the cross, signifying the City of God. They are ultimately on the side of the angels, MacIan knowingly and Turnbull unknowingly.

At its core, *The Ball and the Cross* is a reflection of the inexorable bond between clarity and charity. It shows that reason is inseparable from love. When we succumb to hatred of our enemies, we are already on the wrong side, even if we are saying the right thing. Chesterton was always arguing but he never quarreled. May we learn to do the same.

---

[1] G. K. Chesterton, *The Man Who Was Thursday*, in vol. 6 of *The Collected Works of G. K. Chesterton*, comp. Denis J. Conlon (San Francisco: Ignatius Press, 1991), 539.

[2] Ibid.

39

The Waste Land

The Waste Land by T. S. Eliot is probably the most influential poem of the twentieth century and one of the least understood. Published in 1922, it was perceived at the time as being a jarring and iconoclastic modernist attack on tradition. One reviewer described it as a "mad medley" and "so much waste paper".[1] Another thought it depicted "a world, or a mind, in disaster and mocking its despair", adding that it expressed "the toppling of aspirations, the swift disintegration of accepted stability, the crash of an ideal".[2] Its cultural impact was certainly very divisive. The modernist *avant garde* gazed in awe at its many layers of allusive meaning; the old guard claimed that the layers were not so much allusive as an illusion, suspecting that the emperor had no clothes. The pessimism of its language and the libertine nature of its form accentuated the polarized reaction. The detractors included poetic traditionalists, such as G. K. Chesterton, C. S. Lewis, and Alfred Noyes, none of whom were aware of Eliot's own deep traditionalism, which would only become apparent a few years later with his embrace of Anglo-Catholicism and his description of himself as being a Catholic, a royalist, and a classicist. It was

---

[1] *Manchester Guardian*, October 31, 1923.
[2] *Times Literary Supplement*, September 20, 1923.

not until his death more than forty years later that a more balanced perspective would emerge of the cultural impact that the misreading of *The Waste Land* had caused. The obituary to Eliot in *The Times* conveys such a perspective:

> Its presentation of disillusionment and the disintegration of values, catching the mood of the time, made it the poetic gospel of the post-war intelligentsia; at the time, however, few either of its detractors [or] of its admirers saw through the surface innovations and the language of despair to the deep respect for tradition and the keen moral sense which underlay them.[3]

It is ironic that the key that unlocks *The Waste Land* is Eliot's great admiration for Dante. "You cannot ... understand the *Inferno*", Eliot had written, "without the *Purgatorio* and the *Paradiso*."[4] The "disgust" that Dante shows in the *Inferno* "is completed and explained only by the last canto of the *Paradiso*.... The contemplation of the horrid or sordid or disgusting, by an artist, is the necessary and negative aspect of the impulse toward the pursuit of beauty."[5] It is, therefore, in the light of the peace and resurrection at the end of *The Waste Land* that the earlier infernal and purgatorial aspects of the poem are to be seen.

The epigraph at the beginning of the poem sets the scene and the prophetic tone with its reference to the Cumaean Sibyl, the most famous of the ancient prophetesses whom the Greeks and Romans consulted about the future. She is described at length in Virgil's *Aeneid*, in

---

[3] *The Times*, January 5, 1965.
[4] T. S. Eliot, *The Sacred Wood* (London: Methuen, 1960), 168–69.
[5] Ibid.

which she shows Aeneas how to enter the underworld, and she is featured in Virgil's *Fourth Eclogue*, in which she delivers a prophecy that theologians would later interpret as a foreshadowing of the birth of Christ. The Cumaean Sibyl, in this sense, can be seen as a figure of John the Baptist, as one who cries in the wilderness, in the wasteland, prophesying the coming of Christ.

The poem itself is divided into five parts. Part I, "The Burial of the Dead", begins with an allusion to Chaucer's *Canterbury Tales* that sets the scene of pilgrimage. There then follow a heap of biblical allusions from the Old Testament, references to Job, Ezekiel, Ecclesiastes, and Isaiah, which provides the penitential atmosphere:

> What are the roots that clutch, what branches grow
> Out of this stony rubbish? Son of man,
> You cannot say, or guess, for you know only
> A heap of broken images.
>
> (lines 19–22)[6]

In these few lines, echoing intertextually with cautionary verses from Scripture, the image of the waste land of modernity is laid out before us. The "stony rubbish" of modern culture enables no roots of tradition to clutch and, therefore, no beautiful cultural fruits can be found on branches that cannot grow. Instead we are left with nothing but incohesive and incoherent fragments, a heap of broken images. The poem's fragmented form is itself a reflection of the fragmented formlessness of the modernity it satirizes and reproaches. As for its moral purpose, it is to show us something beyond our narcissistic selves:

[6] T. S. Eliot, "The Waste Land" (New York: Boni and Liveright, 1922).

And I will show you something different from either
Your shadow at morning striding behind you
Or your shadow at evening rising to meet you;
I will show you fear in a handful of dust.

                                        (lines 27–30)

The Waste Land is, therefore, a memento mori, a reminder of death—ashes to ashes, dust to dust—and the Four Last Things to which such a reminder points: death, judgment, heaven, and hell.

The final section of Part I introduces a new motif of the "unreal city", an image of modernity severed from reality by accretions of artificiality or what we might now call virtual reality. Part I ends with the poet pointing the finger at the reader in its quoting of the final line of Baudelaire's famous poem "To the Reader": "You! hypocrite lecteur!—mon semblable,—mon frère!" (You! hypocrite reader! My semblance,—my brother!) What we are reading is aimed at us. It's personal. We are hypocrites who need to look at the plank in our own eye.

Parts II and III present tableaux of the lust and decadence of rich and poor alike, including intertextual allusions to Shakespeare's Cleopatra, to Elizabeth I and the Earl of Leicester, to a middle-class typist and the "young man carbuncular" (line 231) to whom she sacrifices her virginity, after which he bestows "one final patronizing kiss" (line 247) before taking his leave, and to working-class people in a pub who discuss sex within the context of abortion and other manifestations of the culture of death.

Part III ends the section on decadence and lust with a reference to St. Augustine's *Confessions* ("O Lord Thou pluckest me out" [line 309]), signifying and prophesying the turning point of the poem from the inferno of modern fatuity and vacuity to the purgatorial cleansing of the passions.

Part IV is entitled "Death by Water", offering a further memento mori but, beyond that, a promise of the death and resurrection wrought by baptism.

Part V begins with the barren and arid image of the desert and the thirst for water it induces. There then follows an allusion to Christ on the road to Emmaus and a listing of the "falling towers" of the Cities of Man:

> Falling towers
> Jerusalem Athens Alexandria
> Vienna London
> Unreal
>
> (lines 374–77)

All the major centers of civilization, which have been pivotal to human history, are listed as fallen and unreal except for Rome, which is omitted ostentatiously. Only the Eternal City remains. Rome has not fallen, nor is it unreal.

The poem culminates and climaxes in the coming of the much-needed and much-desired rain, a symbol of grace, and "the awful daring of a moment's surrender" (line 404) that is the acceptance of faith. As the thunder proclaims the need for sacrifice, compassion, and self-control, the poet ends with gratitude for the peace that passeth all understanding.

40

Kristin Lavransdatter

No book on great literature would be complete without due attention being given to Sigrid Undset, a Norwegian novelist and convert to the faith, who would be awarded the Nobel Prize for Literature in 1928, four years after her reception into the Church. Her two most celebrated works are *Kristin Lavransdatter* and *The Master of Hestviken*, both of which are multivolume historical epics set in medieval Norway, the first of which was published in three parts between 1920 and 1922 and the latter in four parts between 1925 and 1927.

Although *Kristin Lavransdatter*, unlike *The Master of Hestviken*, was written prior to Undset's reception into the Church, the seeds of conversion are evident in the tone and tenor of the story, in its moral fabric, and in the all-pervasive atmosphere of Thomistic ethical reality.

The novel's plot follows the trials and tribulations of the eponymous heroine from her childhood to her death. The young Kristin betrays her family, and especially her wise and holy father, in her succumbing to willful passion and its woeful and complex consequences. The reader winces as the young and headstrong girl makes mistake after mistake, failing to follow with faith and reason the path of wisdom and virtue. She learns from her mistakes, sometimes painfully slowly, by learning to live with their consequences, loving even as she is often deprived of the love she needs. It is as a wife and mother, embracing the struggle and suffering of married life, that she comes of age, seasoned by the experience of a life lived for others.

The novel is rooted in Norwegian history, of which Undset had a thoroughgoing knowledge, and in the spirit of the Norse sagas, which she also knew well. The action is pedestrian in the best sense of the word, proceeding at the slow and steady pace of the seasons of the year and at the speed with which a person can travel either on foot or on horseback. Such pacing allows the reader to enter fully into the time in which the story is set by entering into the time taken by the characters themselves. This slows us down so that we can see with eyes unblurred by the pace and frenzy of modern life, inviting an unhurried, contemplative approach to the unfolding of events as they transpire. This aspect of Undset's novel might remind some readers of the perambulations of the Fellowship of the Ring in Tolkien's classic, which is imbued with the same preindustrial pacing as *Kristin Lavransdatter* and shares the same heroic spirit of the Norse sagas, the love of which was shared by both authors and the influence of which served each of them in terms of inspiration and aspiration.

Although the pacing and historical and cultural backdrop might suggest analogies with Middle-earth, the development of character and the connection between actions and their consequences might invite parallels with the novels of Jane Austen or perhaps with *The Betrothed* by Manzoni. Certainly, Undset's characters suffer the consequences of their actions and come to wisdom through living with such consequences as do the characters in Austen's novels and Manzoni's masterpiece.

The power and profundity of *Kristen Lavransdatter* has as its source the author's profound understanding of the meaning of life. This manifests itself in the manner in which her characters grapple with reality as a quest for that deeper meaning which the author already grasps. Readers of the novel grapple with this reality also, empathizing and sympathizing with Kristin as she learns to cope with an unfaithful and weak-willed husband and as she learns the meaning of life and love through her experience of being a mother in hard and distressful circumstances. The power of the story and Undset's power as a storyteller are evident in the way in which the reader is drawn into the very presence of the angst and anger of the situations in which Kristin finds herself. We suffer with the eponymous heroine as she hungers for true happiness, finding solace in the raising of her children but feeling unfulfilled in the sense that she lacks the fullness of life. It is only as she matures, painfully slowly, that she begins to find and feel the fullness of the love that had always eluded her.

We will conclude with a few words about Undset's other works. Her other great historical saga, *The Master of Hestviken*, is also set in medieval Norway and follows the sorrowful fortunes of Olav Audunssøn who, like Shakespeare's Lear, is more sinned against than sinning. As with Kristin Lavransdatter, the key characters gain consolation amid the maelstrom of life's misfortunes in their Catholic faith and are fortified by the wise counsel of saintly bishops and priests.

Sigrid Undset's later works were mostly set in contemporary Norway but echoed the historical sagas in their portrayal of characters who learn from their mistakes, growing in sanity and sanctity thereby. These include *Ida Elizabeth* and *The Wild Orchid*, the latter of which tells the story of Paul Selmer and his slow and faltering journey toward the Catholic Church. An unabashed "novel of conversion", *The Wild Orchid* charts the protagonist's journey from skepticism to faith amid a backdrop of failed relationships. At the novel's culmination, Paul has still not taken the decisive step to submit himself to Holy Mother Church, but he appears on the brink of doing so. His final crossing of the threshold is told in the sequel, *The Burning Bush*, which leads him deeper into the mystery of life through the embrace of death, the ultimate paradox of the Christian life.

Sigrid Undset's legacy as a novelist is rooted in the realism of the scholastic philosophy of which she was a diligent student. Her novels expose the shallowness of relativism and exhibit the deepest metaphysical understanding of the bedrock morality on which all human life and society is founded. She sees the real world in which people face the bitter consequences of selfish choices and in which suffering is unavoidable, yet potentially redemptive. She sees this and shows it to her readers with a crystalline clarity enriched with Christian charity. At its deepest, her fiction shows us that the acceptance and embrace of suffering is not merely the beginning of wisdom, which it is, but also, and paradoxically, the path to peace and lasting joy.

41

C

C is one of the longest works featured in this book, weighing in at over seven hundred pages, as well as having the shortest title. It is also neglected and little known as is its author, Maurice Baring. It would be well, therefore, to say a little about the author and his importance before we proceed to what is arguably his finest work.

Maurice Baring was born in 1874, the same year as his good friend G. K. Chesterton. A convert to the faith, he was received into the Church in 1909. Although he is a very fine poet, he is better known as a novelist. Between the two world wars, he wrote several popular and highly regarded novels. These include *Robert Peckham*, a historical novel set during the Tudor terror of the sixteenth century, and several novels set in contemporary England and Europe. Hilaire Belloc considered one of Baring's novels, *Cat's Cradle*, to be "a great masterpiece ... the best story of a woman's life that I know".[1] G. K. Chesterton wrote that he had been "much uplifted" by Baring's novel *The Coat without Seam*, comparing it "with much of the very good Catholic work now being done, especially in France".[2]

[1] Robert Speaight, ed., *Letters from Hilaire Belloc* (London: Hollis and Carter, 1958), 213.
[2] Emma Letley, *Maurice Baring: A Citizen of Europe* (London: Constable, 1991), 217.

François Mauriac, one of the finest novelists of the Catholic literary revival in France to which Chesterton was referring, was a great admirer of Baring's novels. "What I most admire about Baring's work", Mauriac said, "is the sense he gives you of the penetration of grace."[3] Baring was "too moved to speak"[4] when he learned of Mauriac's praise.

Baring was inadvertently describing himself in the description of a character in *The Coat without Seam*: "Everything about him ... gave one the impression of centuries and hidden stores of pent-up civilization."[5] He knew Latin, Greek, French, German, Italian, Russian, and Danish, and he was widely read in the literature of all these languages. Reading his work is like stepping into the presence of someone who walks on a crystal floor of culture above our heads.

As the aforementioned quote by Mauriac might suggest, Baring enjoyed great success in France. Ten of his books were translated into French, with one—*Daphne Adeana*—going through twenty-three reprintings. His novels were also translated into Czech, Dutch, German, Hungarian, Italian, Spanish, and Swedish.

C, published in 1924, received the highest of praise from the French novelist André Maurois, who wrote that no book had given him such pleasure since his reading of Tolstoy, Proust, and certain novels by E. M. Forster.

As we begin to discuss the novel, it might be good to start with an explanation of its title. "C" is the nickname given to the novel's protagonist, the Honorable Caryl

[3] Laura Lovat, *Maurice Baring: A Postscript* (London: Hollis and Carter, 1947), 4–5.

[4] Ibid.

[5] Maurice Baring, *The Coat Without Seam* (Looe, Cornwall: House of Stratus, 2001), 252.

Bramsley, by his family and friends. The second son and fourth child of Lord and Lady Hengrave, C moves in an aristocratic world of opulence, high culture, and low morals. A precocious child who struggles to adapt to adulthood, he is torn between the two types of "love" that are ever at war in the human heart. The first is the call to caritas, the sacrificing of the self for the beloved; the other is the pursuit of eros, the sacrificing of the beloved on the altar erected to the self. It is this war which wages itself relentlessly in C's own selfish heart.

The higher calling of caritas is epitomized by C's thwarted relationship with the aptly and symbolically named Beatrice. Meanwhile, his lower appetites hunger after the seductive and flirtatious Leila, the beautiful wife of a successful diplomat.

On the surface, the religious element is present in the presence of Beatrice, a devout and virtuous Catholic, but the deepest spiritual dimension is subsumed within the very depths of cultural sensibility and the breathtaking breadth of intertextual interplay with which Baring breathes ethical and aesthetic life into the weavings and wanderings of the plot. We see how C's early infatuation with Romantic poetry in general, and the poetry of Shelley in particular, impacts his philosophy of life and love. We see how his dabbling with the diabolism of the French Decadents intoxicates his aesthetic sensibility, poisoning his innocence with the suggestive promises of pride. We see how his reading weakens and finally destroys his already weak and faltering Christian faith. We see how his descent into atheism is seen as a liberation of the spirit from the constraints of Christian morality.

Throughout the novel, the music of Wagner provides a hauntingly recurring soundtrack, a leitmotif of doom-laden desire and gloom-laden desolation. The Wagnerian influence on C's character is reflected in a sonnet that Baring wrote entitled "Wagner":

> O strange awakening to a world of gloom,
> And baffled moonbeams and delirious stars,
> Of souls that moan behind forbidden bars,
> And waving forests swept by wings of doom.[6]

This evokes the "strange awakening to a world of gloom" that the discovery of Wagner has on C, a discovery that dooms him to the pursuit of dark and delirious delights, the fruit of which is frustration. Again, Baring's sonnet speaks for the novel's protagonist:

> O restless soul, for ever seeking bliss,
> Athirst for ever and unsatisfied.

There is, however, a powerful antidote to this recurring Wagnerian siren call in the perennial metaphorical presence of Dante throughout the novel. Seeing this sublime and subliminal presence enables us to perceive the intertextual counterpoint that Dante's presence represents. With the beatific Beatrice providing the clue, we can see how C is a Dante figure who has allowed himself to wander into the dark wood of sin, a slave to his sinful appetites. And of course, insofar as C is a Dante figure, in the context of Dante's character in the *Divine Comedy*, he is also an Everyman figure and therefore a cautionary figure. C shows us ourselves or the selves we might become if we choose to pursue certain "loves" at the expense of others. The question that the novel asks and finally answers is whether C will respond to the higher call to which Beatrice

[6] Maurice Baring, *Collected Poems* (London: William Heinemann, 1925), 63.

beckons him or whether he will remain, like Paolo in the *Inferno*, a restless soul, forever seeking bliss, athirst forever and forever unsatisfied.

In our uncivilized age, it is perhaps inevitable that the civilized brilliance of Maurice Baring should have been eclipsed by the polluting smog of uncultured mediocrity. For as long as the light of civilization dwindles, so will the reputation of this most civilized of writers. One might hope that the inevitable demise of burned-out nihilism will lead to a resurrection of all that is good, true, and beautiful in literature. If such a resurrection happens, Maurice Baring's work will once again be as widely read and enjoyed as it once was.

42

Brideshead Revisited

The deeply Catholic spirit of *Brideshead Revisited* was encapsulated by its author, Evelyn Waugh, in the preface he wrote to the second edition of his greatest novel. The novel's theme was, he wrote, "the operation of divine grace on a group of diverse but closely connected characters".[1] He added that such a theme "was perhaps presumptuously large, but I make no apology for it".[2]

Taking Waugh at his word, in the knowledge that ignoring the authorial authority is always perilous to an understanding of the work, we must acknowledge from the outset that *Brideshead Revisited* is supernatural to the core of its very being. Its chief protagonist is not any of the human physical characters but is the invisible hand of providence, which provides the grace that is necessary for the conversion of souls. It is this invisible hand of grace which guides the plot, writing straight with the crooked lines and lives of the flawed human characters.

The very title of the novel offers a clue to its supernatural identity. Brideshead, the name of a stately manor house, the home of an aristocratic and dysfunctional Catholic family, is clearly symbolic, the bride's head being the

---

[1] Evelyn Waugh, *Brideshead Revisited* (New York: Back Bay Books, 2020), ix.
[2] Ibid.

bridegroom, a signifier for Christ Himself. "Brideshead Revisited" is, therefore, Christ revisited. This supernatural dimension is emphasized by the novel's liturgical structure, the first part ending metaphorically on Good Friday and the novel itself ending metaphorically on Easter Sunday.

The "closely connected characters" weaving and wending their way through the pages of the novel are the various members of the aristocratic Flyte family. Lord Marchmain, the head of the family, has deserted his wife and children and has taken up residence in Venice with a concubine. Lady Marchmain, the deserted wife, is stoically and piously Catholic but somewhat aloof. Lord Brideshead, the eldest son, is a solid and faithful Catholic, steeped in scholastic philosophy and Jesuit spirituality, but is socially awkward and inept. Sebastian, the younger son, is the very opposite of his brother. He is a faltering Catholic whose faith is not rooted in reason but in an emotion-driven romantic aestheticism. He is, however, very charming, at least superficially. Julia, the elder daughter, is physically beautiful and very self-centered. Like Sebastian, she is irked by the demands that the practice of the faith places upon her, resenting its inhibiting of her "freedom". The youngest child, Cordelia, lacks her sister's physical beauty but has the piety and the faith that Julia lacks. This is how Sebastian describes his family:

> We're a mixed family religiously. Brideshead and Cordelia are both fervent Catholics; he's miserable, she's bird-happy; Julia and I are half-heathen; I am happy, I rather think Julia isn't; Mummy is popularly believed to be a saint and Papa is excommunicated—and I wouldn't know which of them was happy. Anyway, however you look at it, happiness doesn't seem to have much to do with it, and that's all I want.[3]

[3] Ibid., 98–99.

Apart from allowing the narrator, Charles Ryder, to know the Flyte family better, Sebastian's words also introduce the riddle of happiness that the novel seeks to solve. What is happiness? How is it to be attained? Once attained, how is it to be retained and maintained?

Charles Ryder, the narrator, is the other key character, whose voice must be understood if we are to understand the novel itself. The narrative voice, introduced in the Prologue, is one that speaks with apparent disillusionment. "Here at the age of thirty-nine I began to be old.... Here my last love died. There was nothing remarkable in the manner of its death."[4] It is this middle-aged and jaded voice that speaks throughout the novel, recounting the past with the wisdom of experience. This is most evident when we are told of how Charles turns his back on Brideshead for what he thinks will be the last time:

> "I have left behind illusion," I said to myself. "Henceforth I live in a world of three dimensions—with the aid of my five senses."
>
> I have since learned that there is no such world; but then, as the car turned out of sight of the house, I thought it took no finding, but lay all about me at the end of the avenue.[5]

In this brief passage, we see the subtly subversive voice of the middle-aged narrator sitting in judgment on the naiveté of his younger self. In turning his back on Brideshead, the young Charles believed that he was turning his back on what he presumed was an illusionary supernatural cosmos. Henceforth, he would believe only in the three physical dimensions as perceived by his five physical senses.

[4] Ibid., 5.
[5] Ibid., 195.

Everything other than this was an illusion. The older Charles has learned, however, that "there is no such world" as that in which the naive atheist believes. It is the world of the materialist that is the world of illusion. The older Charles has seen through the disillusionment of his youth and has become disillusioned with it!

We come to understand that Charles Ryder's disillusionment with his younger self's atheism is the fruit of the wisdom of experience and especially of the wisdom of the experience of suffering. Two powerful metaphors are employed to evoke the role of suffering in bringing selfish souls to their senses. The first is "the twitch upon the thread", the title of the final part of the book, which is taken from a Father Brown story by G. K. Chesterton. The thread is the divine grace that weaves its way throughout the story, as Waugh had proclaimed in the Prologue. The twitch upon the thread is the moment of suffering when the wandering soul is jerked violently from its chosen destructive path by the hook of God's own suffering love.

The other metaphor is that of an avalanche that is employed as a recurring motif in the final chapters of the book. Charles likens the happiness that he and Julia are seeking in the midst of a cold and loveless world to a trapper in the warmth of an arctic hut. Outside the snow is piling up against the door as the blizzard rages. Inside they are warm, "until quite soon, when the wind dropped and the sun came out on the ice slopes and the thaw set in, a block would move, slide and tumble, high above, gather way, gather weight, till the whole hillside seemed to be falling, and the little lighted place would crash open and splinter and disappear, rolling with the avalanche into the ravine."[6]

[6] Ibid., 357.

The paradox that these powerful metaphors evoke is that suffering is essential to the growth of the soul into the depths of the truly self-sacrificial love to which it is called. Health is not the avoidance of suffering but the acceptance of suffering. It is only in such acceptance that health, healing, and suffering can be united in a triune synthesis known as holiness. It is this wisdom that Waugh weaves with the invisible thread of grace that he evokes. It is this wisdom that answers the riddle of happiness that *Brideshead Revisited* sets out to answer. True happiness is not possible without the health and healing that comes only through suffering. This is the wisdom that Charles Ryder has learned by the end of the novel. In losing everything, he has attained a deeper happiness than he had ever known. He is disillusioned with his own disillusionment and disenchanted with his own disenchantment. It is, therefore, a reenchanted Charles Ryder who is described in the novel's concluding sentence as "looking unusually cheerful today".

43

The Hobbit

J. R. R. Tolkien said of his magnum opus, *The Lord of the Rings*, that it was, "of course, a fundamentally religious and Catholic work".[1] The same could be said of his earlier work, *The Hobbit*.

Although *The Hobbit* can be seen as a prequel, of sorts, to *The Lord of the Rings*, its relative levitas stands in idiosyncratic contrast to the gravitas of the latter work. This is due to the fact that *The Hobbit* was written specifically as a children's book, whereas *The Lord of the Rings* outgrew its originally intended role as a sequel. As Tolkien wrote the latter book, it took on epic and mythic proportions, "growing up" into adulthood with respect to genre.

The "fundamentally religious and Catholic" dimension of *The Hobbit* is to be found in its treatment of the "dragon sickness", which serves the same catalytic moral purpose as does the power of the Ring in *The Lord of the Rings*. Essentially the dragon sickness is the possessiveness of things, especially gold and gems, which has a detrimental effect on the moral health of the one afflicted with it, as well as a destructive impact on others.

[1] Humphrey Carpenter, *The Letters of J. R. R. Tolkien* (London: George Allen & Unwin, 1981), 172.

As the name of the sickness would suggest, dragons are particularly prone to the dragon sickness. Smaug squats on his hoard of treasure, jealously guarding it. He is trapped by it. He cannot leave for fear that a thief might steal something in his absence. Ironically, he is a prisoner of the very thing he is guarding. He is possessed by his possessiveness of his possessions.

As the moral applicability of Smaug's possessiveness suggests, the dragon sickness does not only afflict dragons. It affects people. It affects dwarves. It affects hobbits.

At the beginning of the story, Bilbo Baggins is suffering from the dragon sickness, though he doesn't realize it until later, and nor do we. It's through the experience of the sufferings and dangers of the quest, and the self-sacrificial spirit that such suffering and danger enkindle, that Bilbo comes to understand why the adventure was necessary for his own moral growth and maturity.

When we first meet Bilbo, he is a creature of comfort addicted to the creature comforts. He is squatting on all the comfortable and comforting things with which he has surrounded himself. We are told in the very opening paragraph of the story that Bilbo lived in "a hobbit-hole, and that means comfort".

Like Smaug, the hobbit is possessed by his possessiveness of his possessions. The dragon lives under the mountain; the hobbit lives under a hill (indeed, the hobbit lives in a part of Hobbiton called Underhill). The difference between the dragon suffering from the dragon sickness and the hobbit suffering from the same affliction is, therefore, merely one of scale (pun intended!).

The reason that Gandalf tells Bilbo that the adventure with the dwarves will be good for Bilbo, the physical dangers notwithstanding, is that Bilbo needs to gain a detachment from his material possessions by detaching himself from them. He needs to escape from the comforts of home in order to experience the fullness of life, which involves the willing embrace of discomfort and suffering as a means of self-sacrificially serving others. In short and in sum, Bilbo Baggins has to learn how to love; he needs to learn the necessity of laying down his life for his friends. The politeness of domesticity is not enough; he must take up his cross. He must leave the comforts of home to embark on the adventure of life, which is not merely a journey but a pilgrimage. It is the path of holiness, understood allegorically, the quest for heaven.

When Bilbo returns home after the adventure, the kettle on the hearth sounds sweeter than ever because he is no longer possessed by it. He is free from his addiction to the comforts of home. He has recovered from the dragon sickness. "My dear Bilbo!" Gandalf exclaims. "Something is the matter with you! You are not the hobbit that you were."[2] Bilbo has changed. Indeed, he has changed so radically that the only real word for it is conversion. It is, therefore, symbolically appropriate that he is "presumed dead"[3] by his neighbors, his having been away for so long. His return home is a return from the dead. A resurrection. Bilbo had learned to die to himself that he might live for others. It is the death that leads to the only life that matters, a life of grace in Christ.

At its deepest level, The Hobbit can be seen as a parabolic commentary on the words from St. Matthew's Gospel (6:21) that where our treasure is, there our heart will be also. It is in this sense that The Hobbit can be seen as "a fundamentally religious and Catholic work".

[2] J. R. R. Tolkien, The Hobbit (London: Harper Collins, 1988), 281.
[3] Ibid., 282.

44

The Lord of the Rings

According to its author, J. R. R. Tolkien, *The Lord of the Rings* "is, of course, a fundamentally religious and Catholic work",[1] as mentioned in the previous chapter. This might puzzle or mystify many people. There is, after all, no mention of Christ or His Church anywhere in its thousand or so pages.

The Catholic dimension is subsumed within the work, hidden under the literal surface in multifarious ways. Most specifically, the key to understanding the religious dimension of the work is to be found in the date on which the Ring is destroyed. This is March 25, a hugely significant date on the Christian calendar and perhaps the most significant date of all. Most Catholics will know that March 25 is the date of the Annunciation, the date on which the Word becomes flesh, the date of the Incarnation, when God becomes man. Since human life begins at conception, not birth, the Annunciation is more important than Christmas.

Many people, even Catholics, will not know that March 25 was also widely believed by those in the early and medieval Church to be the historical date of the Crucifixion. Since Good Friday is a movable feast, we don't assign a

[1] Humphrey Carpenter, *The Letters of J. R. R. Tolkien* (London: George Allen & Unwin, 1981), 172.

particular date to the death of Christ, yet He died on one particular date in history. This date, according to tradition, was March 25. Tolkien, a medieval scholar, knew this and used it as the inspiration for the assigning of this date to the Ring's destruction.

The Annunciation, taken together with the Crucifixion and Resurrection, constitutes our redemption, our liberation from the power of sin. Original Sin is the one sin to rule them all and in the darkness bind them. The Ring is the one ring to rule them all and in the darkness bind them. The one Sin and the one Ring are both destroyed on the same significant date.

The power of the Ring is, therefore, an allegorical depiction of the power of sin. The act of putting on the Ring is the act of sin. The Ring wearer is living in sin. He becomes invisible to the good world that God has made, excommunicating himself from the light of goodness, truth, and beauty, but becomes more visible to the demonic Sauron who rules wherever the shadow of sin shields the sinner from the light.

On the other hand, the one who bears the weight of the Ring, the weight of sin, without succumbing to its power, is bearing the cross. The Ring bearer is the cross bearer. In this sense, Frodo Baggins is both a Christ figure and a figure of one who follows Christ by taking up his cross. It is, therefore, not surprising that Frodo leaves Rivendell on December 25 and arrives at Mount Doom (Golgotha) on March 25, his journey matching the life of Christ from the Nativity to the Crucifixion.

In addition to this overarching Christological and cosmological dimension of Frodo's quest, *The Lord of the Rings* contains a couple of other dexterously suggestive figures of Christ. First is Gandalf, whose death and resurrection is accompanied by his transfiguration from being Gandalf the

Grey to Gandalf the White; second is Aragorn, whose true kingship gives him the power to descend into the paths of the dead, releasing the dead themselves from their curse.

Apart from the aforementioned Christ figures, Tolkien's epic also presents several Everyman figures, evocative of Tolkien's insistence in his famous essay "On Fairy-Stories" that fairytales hold up "a mirror to man". They show us ourselves. This is most evident in the character of Boromir, who is the official representative of the race of men in the Fellowship of the Ring. He is there on our behalf. It is he who betrays the Fellowship, seeking to use the power of the Ring to save his own people. This willingness to use evil means to a purportedly good end leads only to the ultimate triumph of evil because sin can't be used to defeat sin. Boromir repents and lays down his life for his friends. His final exchange of words with Aragorn reflects the form of the sacrament of penance, Aragorn acting *in persona Christi* as Boromir confesses his sin.

Faramir serves as another Everyman figure, as is evident analogically by his being Boromir's brother. Faramir declares that he would not pick up the Ring if he saw it lying at the side of the road. He also says that he wouldn't snare even an orc with a falsehood—not the smallest lie to the devil himself.

A third rather sobering Everyman figure is Gollum, whose addiction to the power of the Ring serves to highlight the shriveling and shrinking of the soul if it surrenders itself to the decadent quest for "self-empowerment".

Much more could and should be said about the multi-faceted and multifarious applicable meanings that emerge from this timeless classic. In essence, however, or in a nutshell, the key is to be found in the date on which the Ring is destroyed. From this, as from an acorn, Tolkien's tree of tales reaches for the heavens.

45

Till We Have Faces

Some of the works selected for this book might appear somewhat idiosyncratic or even quixotic. Little-known works have rarely but occasionally been included, and much better-known works have been excluded. Wherever a relatively obscure title has been selected, a rational justification has been offered for its inclusion. As for the exclusion of better-known books, this is simply unavoidable. This book would need to include hundreds of these "nutshell" nuggets for sins of omission to be avoided.

The preceding preamble serves as a preliminary defense of the inclusion of a work by C.S. Lewis that is neither the best known or most read of his multifarious works. Its inclusion is the consequence of a process of elimination. As this is a book on literature, Lewis' many works of nonfiction do not really qualify. Any of the books in the Narnia series warrants inclusion but none to the exclusion of the others. Since it would be disproportionate to have seven separate "nutshells" on each of the books, and since children's books, with the exception of *The Hobbit*, have not been included, it seemed best to consider other titles instead. The same logic applies to the Space Trilogy. Any and all of these books warrant inclusion but none to the exclusion of the others.

This process of elimination having been followed, we are left with a mere handful of titles from which to choose.

Of those that remain, *Till We Have Faces* is indubitably the best. And this is not only the considered opinion of the present author; it is also the considered opinion of C. S. Lewis himself. He called it "much my best book" and "far and away the best I have written". It was also the "favorite of all my books".[1] Since the great man himself considered it both his best and his favorite, no further justification for its inclusion instead of his many other great works need be given.

The foregoing having been said, it must also be admitted that it is the most difficult of Lewis' books to understand and, in consequence, is not the most popular. The first difficulty is that it is a retelling of the ancient myth of Cupid and Psyche. It is helpful, therefore, though certainly not necessary, for readers to have some knowledge of the inspirational source that fired Lewis' imagination when writing *Till We Have Faces*, which is subtitled *A Myth Retold*.

In essence, the story focuses on the estrangement between friends or family members following religious conversion. Orual deeply loves her younger half-sister, Psyche, and the two develop a close bond in childhood. Orual is disturbed and then angered when Psyche claims to be living in a happy marriage with the god she had been "sacrificed" to in a religious ritual. Although Psyche clearly believes that she is in a beautiful palace, it is invisible to Orual, who can see nothing but barren countryside. As with the religious convert, Psyche now sees reality very differently from her sister, who is unable to see that which is inaccessible to the nonbeliever. What makes matters worse is Orual's obsessive and possessive love for Psyche.

---

[1] Walter Hooper, ed., *The Collected Letters of C. S. Lewis*, vol. 3 (San Francisco: Harper San Francisco, 2007), 1148.

She resents Psyche's happiness because it has placed a barrier between them. She blames the gods for taking Psyche from her. She is so full of anger that she refuses to acknowledge the existence of Psyche's palace even when granted a glimpse of it. She explains the vision away. Orual's anger turns to hatred of the gods and of Psyche. (Those wishing a deeper understanding of the destructiveness of possessive love should read *Till We Have Faces* in conjunction with those parts of Lewis' *The Great Divorce* that deal with the domineering self-centered wife and the domineering self-centered mother whose possessiveness prevents them from willing the good of the beloved.)

Another facet of *Till We Have Faces* is the tension between "reason" and "religion" as made manifest in the disagreements between a character called the Fox, a Greek slave steeped in the philosophy of his homeland, and the Priest of Ungit, a pagan priest steeped in the rites and traditions of his religion. The Fox is skeptical of all religious claims that transcend his philosophical rationalism; the Priest is skeptical of philosophy because of the limitations it seems to place on numinous or transcendent truth. This dynamic tension creates a dialectic between faith and reason that highlights the dangers of the divorce of one from the other.

One reason that *Till We Have Faces* is less popular than many of Lewis' other books is that it is harder to understand. It is Lewis at his least didactic and most literary. The meaning does not float on the surface or near the surface, as with many of his other works, but is submerged and subsumed in the story itself. Lewis is not preaching or teaching. He is simply telling a story or retelling an old story in his own inimitable way.

Paradoxically, *Till We Have Faces* is a work about masks that wears a mask itself. This is evident in its very title, which many have found confusing. It is taken from the words of Orual, who had shielded herself from reality and from life, and from god and neighbor, by the wearing of masks, placing a barrier between herself and others. In the final chapter, in a moment of epiphany, she says the following: "How can they [the gods] meet us face to face till we have faces?"[2] This is the question that *Till We Have Faces* asks us. If we insist on living in a self-constructed masquerade, wearing masks as false identities to hide ourselves from ourselves and others, we will not be able to see the splendor of the truth that is beyond ourselves. This is made clear in Lewis' own explanation of the title and its significance:

> How can they (i.e. the gods) meet us face to face till we have faces? The idea was that a human being must become real before it can expect to receive any message from the superhuman; that is, it must be speaking with its own voice (not one of its borrowed voices), expressing its actual desires (not what it imagines that it desires), being for good or ill itself, not any mask, veil or *persona*.[3]

Throughout the story, Orual is prevented by her own pride from seeing reality. She needs her pride to be broken in humiliation so that she can gain the humility necessary to come to her senses. It is only then that she can sense and see the deeper reality that had eluded her.

We'll conclude with a descent into the vulgar vernacular of the modern voice. The ultimate meaning of *Till We Have Faces* is that we need to get real before we can get reality.

[2] C. S. Lewis, *Till We Have Faces* (Orlando, Florida: Harcourt, 1984), 294.
[3] Walter Hooper, *C. S. Lewis: A Companion and Guide* (London: Fount, 1997), 252.

46

One Day in the Life of Ivan Denisovich

There can be few more worthy winners of the Nobel Prize for Literature than Aleksandr Solzhenitsyn, who illustrates in his life and work the power of literature to transform society.

Born in 1918, only a year after the Bolshevik Revolution had unleashed the terror of communism on the peoples of what would become known as the Soviet Union, Solzhenitsyn would become one of the most influential figures in his nation's quest for freedom from Marxist tyranny.

Sentenced to seven years in the Soviet labor camps for the "crime" of criticizing Josef Stalin in private correspondence, Solzhenitsyn would expose the horrors of the camps in his three-volume magnum opus, *The Gulag Archipelago*, and also in the short novel, *One Day in the Life of Ivan Denisovich*. Whereas the former, which was subtitled *An Experiment in Literary Investigation*, was a sweeping panoramic history of the whole labor camp system, the latter focused on a single day in one particular camp. The former surveyed the landscape of the camps through a literary telescope; the latter placed the day-to-day life of the prisoners under a microscope.

Solzhenitsyn drew on his own personal experience of the camps in his writing of *One Day in the Life*. The fictional camp in which the novel is set is based on a camp in northern Kazakhstan in which Solzhenitsyn had spent part of his sentence, and the novel's eponymous protagonist, Ivan Denisovich Shukhov, bears a certain resemblance to Solzhenitsyn in his characterization. There is, therefore, a quasi-autobiographical dimension to the story.

As the title suggests, the whole action of the novel takes place on one solitary day in the life of the protagonist. In this way, Solzhenitsyn takes the reader into the claustrophobically monotonous life of the prisoners, who follow the same routine, day in, day out, with no seeming end in sight. We experience not merely the claustrophobic monotony but the chilling physical intensity of the experience. We are marched out with the work party in subzero temperatures to a construction site at which Shukhov works as a bricklayer. It's so cold that the bricks must be laid quickly before the mortar freezes.

The reader also feels the pangs of hunger that are a permanent part of the lives of the prisoners. Shukhov's life is spent finding ways to filch or scrounge additional scraps of food, and one of the most memorable parts of the novel is the description of the spiritual, almost sacramental, act of eating the daily rations. We are told, as Shukhov sits down to eat, that

> the sacred moment had come. Shukhov took off his hat and laid it on his knees. He tasted one bowl, he tasted the other. Not bad, there was some fish in it. Generally, the evening skilly was much thinner than at breakfast; if they're to work, prisoners must be fed in the morning; in the evening they'll go to sleep anyway.
>
> He set to. First he only drank the liquid, drank and drank. As it went down, filling his whole body with warmth, all his guts began to flutter inside him at their meeting with that skilly. Goo-ood! There it comes, that brief moment for which a zek [prisoner] lives.

And now Shukhov complained about nothing: neither about the length of his stretch, nor about the length of the day.... This was all he thought about now: we'll survive. We'll stick it out, God grant, till it's over.[1]

A potato had found its way into the bowl, which was unusual, but not much fish, "just a few stray bits of bare backbone.... But you must chew every bone, every fin, to suck the juice out of them, for the juice is healthy. It takes time, of course, but he was in no hurry to go anywhere."[2] Having supped, he resisted the temptation to eat the bread ration. "The bread would do for tomorrow. The belly is a rascal. It doesn't remember how well you treated it yesterday, it'll cry out for more tomorrow."[3]

Apart from detailing the grim and grueling minutiae of the day's rituals and routines, *One Day in the Life* focuses on the relationships of the prisoners with each other and how each of them copes with the degradation of their daily existence.

Tyurin, the leader of the work party, is a survivor. A veteran of the camp, having been sentenced nineteen years earlier for the "crime" of being from an affluent farming family, he is respected by the other prisoners for his fortitude and his courage, the latter of which is tempered prudently to avoid falling foul of the camp guards.

Fetyukov has abandoned all traces of his human dignity in the pursuit of gratifying his appetites, begging shamelessly for food and tobacco. In slavishly serving his body, he has lost his soul.

[1] Aleksandr Solzhenitsyn, *One Day in the Life of Ivan Denisovich* (Harmondsworth, England: Penguin Books, 1963), 121.

[2] Ibid., 122.

[3] Ibid.

At the other extreme is Buynovsky, known as "the Captain" because of his service as a captain in the Soviet navy. A newcomer to the camp, he takes the dignity of his rank too seriously, lacking the necessary submissiveness. If he is to survive in the camps, he must learn to bend without breaking, as Shukhov and Tyurin have learned to do.

Finally, there is the inspirational figure of Alyoshka the Baptist, who is the Christian presence. He is at peace with himself, with his situation, and with his fellow prisoners because he is at peace with God. He embraces his suffering with the hope of final deliverance. He is not merely surviving physically amid the hardship and harshness of his prison sentence but is thriving spiritually. He serves as a witness to the presence of Christ, a light in the darkness.

The final judgment on *One Day in the Life of Ivan Denisovich* does not belong to the literary critics but to the former prisoners of the Soviet labor camps who wrote to Solzhenitsyn following the novel's publication. "I could not sit still", one former prisoner wrote. "I kept leaping up, walking about and imagined all those scenes as taking place in the camp I was in." "When I read it," wrote another, "I literally felt the blast of cold as one leaves the hut for inspection."

Another former prisoner, after declaring that his own life was described exactly in the novel, recounted his riposte to a woman who had criticized the novel for being too depressing: "It's better to have a bitter truth than a sweet lie", he had replied. The final words belong to a woman whose husband had died in the camps:

> I see, I hear this crowd of hungry, freezing creatures, half people, half animals, and amongst them is my husband.... Continue to write, write the truth, even though they won't

print it now! Our floods of tears were not shed in vain—the truth will rise to the surface in this river of tears.[4]

Solzhenitsyn would continue to write. He would continue to speak the bitter truth and to expose the sweetness of the lie. He would be a tireless advocate for the millions who died in the camps and for the millions who mourn them. Ultimately, his words would prove powerful enough to help bring down the Soviet tyranny. Such is the living legacy of this true hero of the twentieth century.

[4] These reactions to the publication of the novella were published originally in Leopold Labedz, ed., *Solzhenitsyn: A Documentary Record* (Harmondsworth, England: Penguin Books, 1974), 48–53.

47

The Violent Bear It Away

Flannery O'Connor is probably best known for her short stories, but she also wrote two novels, *Wise Blood* (1952) and *The Violent Bear It Away* (1960). Her modus operandi as a writer was the employment of violence and the grotesque to shock her readers out of their somnambulant indifference to truth. Such violence and grotesqueness are never used gratuitously but are always pregnant with metaphysical meaning. The murderous violence of the Misfit in the short story "A Good Man Is Hard to Find" serves as an unwitting agent of grace, bringing the grandmother to her knees and her senses, even as it brings her life to an end. In *Wise Blood*, the pathological pride of the Christ-haunted and Christ-hating protagonist reaps such a bitter and embittered harvest of destruction and desolation that the necessity of Christ's presence is implied by the consequences of his absence. The overall effect is akin to Edvard Munch's famous painting, *The Scream*, in which all that is left in the vacuum created by the absence of grace is the vice and viciousness that leads to suicidal despair.

In *The Violent Bear It Away*, O'Connor places the reader in a claustrophobic world in which claustrophobic philosophies close in upon themselves, preventing any real growth in the perception of reality. In doing so, she shows the harmful consequences of sundering faith from reason.

At one end of the philosophical spectrum is the irrational faith of Mason Tarwater, a self-ordained and theologically idiosyncratic "Christian" prophet, who dies at the beginning of the novel, having groomed his orphaned great-nephew, Francis Tarwater, to follow his fanatical prophetic calling. At the other end of the spectrum is the faithless rationalism of Rayber, a fanatically anti-religious schoolteacher and "progressive", who is Francis Tarwater's uncle.

The fourth key character is Bishop, a mentally disabled child who presumably has Down syndrome. It is Bishop's presence that is the leaven that raises the moral dimension of the whole novel. Switching metaphors, he is also the catalyst that enables us to see into the hearts and minds of Rayber and Francis. It is their reaction to his presence that reveals their own personalities and the practical ramifications of their respective philosophies.

Bishop is Rayber's son and Francis' cousin. His mother, Bernice, is an intrusive social worker whom the old man, Mason Tarwater, had dubbed "the welfare woman".[1] The old man, a libertarian with a healthy contempt for progressivism and government intervention, had explained to Francis that God had bestowed his mercy on Bishop by making him "dim-witted",[2] thereby preserving him from being corrupted by the atheism of his parents. Since neither of Bishop's parents would tolerate their son being baptized, Mason Tarwater charges Francis with the "mission"[3] to baptize the child.

Francis Tarwater refuses the mission, considering Bishop to be subhuman and feeling repulsed by him. Ironically, he shares this disrespect for the dignity of Bishop's human personhood with the boy's own father. Rayber resents

[1] Flannery O'Connor, Collected Works, ed. Sally Fitzgerald (New York: Literary Classics of the United States, 1988), 333.
[2] Ibid., 334.
[3] Ibid., 335.

Bishop, seeing no point in him, considering him an imposition and a curse. The most excruciating aspect of the novel is the cruelty and contempt with which Francis and Rayber treat the boy, whose uncomplaining innocence serves as an unwitting foil to their wickedness.

Francis resents and resists Rayber's attempts to "educate" him in the direction of unbelief, but he is equally uncomfortable with belief, seeking to escape from the narrowness of the theology with which he'd been raised. To make matters worse, Francis is also visited at key moments by an invisible "friend", a "voice" that whispers diabolical thoughts into his head. In one of her letters, Flannery O'Connor revealed that this "friend" was in fact the devil himself. It is significant that this diabolical friend speaks to him in the language of rationalist materialism and secularism, tempting him with atheism. The friend plays a key role because of his or its appearance at a critical moment in the story, a moment that is "crucial" in the sense of the ultimate crux of the Crucifixion itself. As for Bishop, he emerges throughout the story, and especially at this crucial moment, as the innocent victim of the sins of others.

It says something of Flannery O'Connor's provocative genius that she can make a psychopathic killer an agent of grace in "A Good Man Is Hard to Find", a wooden leg a symbol of the Cross in "Good Country People", and a child with Down syndrome a Christ figure in *The Violent Bear It Away*.

Perhaps the final words in *The Violent Bear It Away* should be said by the character in the novel who has nothing to say. It is Bishop's powerful silence that speaks loudest.

It has been said, quite truly, that most of us are here to learn, whereas some of are here to teach. Those with Down syndrome are here to teach. This is the lesson that Bishop teaches in *The Violent Bear It Away*.

48

Vinland

Some authors and some books are not as well-known as
they should be. This is indubitably the case with George
Mackay Brown and his tour de force of a novel, *Vinland*.

George Mackay Brown was an Orcadian, a native of the
Orkney Islands, an archipelago to the north of Scotland.
Born in 1921, he was received into the Catholic Church
in 1961. Thereafter, the faith was a palpable presence in
his work, most evocatively in the quasi-autobiographical
short story, "The Tarn and the Rosary". The publication
of *The Year of the Whale* in 1965 established his reputation
as a poet, and the appearance of *A Calendar of Love* in 1967
heralded his arrival as an eminent writer of short stories.

Living the entirety of his life in the relative seclusion
of the Orkneys, except for a brief period as a student in
Edinburgh, Brown's works are imbued with a deep love
for the Orcadian way of life, past and present. Indeed, the
past is always present in his work, in the lives of crofters, fishermen, monks, and Vikings, all of whom live in a
world that is overlaid and underpinned by a deeply religious apprehension and comprehension of eternal verities.
His stories and verse express his passion for the ancient,
the traditional, and the spiritual; they abound with legend and myth, image and symbol, the very language of
mystereality.

The critic Alan Bold, writing of Brown's understanding of the crofters and fishermen who were his neighbors, suggested that such empathy and sympathy made him aware of "the elemental relationship these folk have with, respectively, the soil and the sea".[1] He might also have added that such folk live lives in which the soul is mystically wedded to the soil and the sea. This soul-soil and soul-sea nexus finds expression in the deep theology of place that informs Brown's poetry and poetic prose. Such rootedness in incarnate spirituality explains Brown's reverence for tradition and his conversion to Catholicism, the Old Religion, which was the champion and defender of tradition and its last bastion and refuge. The new anti-traditional religion of what Brown called "our gray twentieth century" was Progress:

> There is a new religion, Progress, in which we all devoutly believe, and it is concerned only with material things in the present and in a vague golden-handed future. It is a rootless utilitarian faith, without beauty or mystery.... The notion of progress is a cancer that makes an elemental community look better, and induces a false euphoria, while it drains the life out of it remorselessly.[2]

This plaintive note, expressed in *An Orkney Tapestry*, Brown's eulogy to the islands of his birth, was taken up by a character in "The Tarn and the Rosary":

> Progress, that's the modern curse. This island is enchanted with the idea of Progress.... This worship of Progress, it will drain the life out of every island and lonely place. In

---

[1] Alan Bold, *George Mackay Brown* (Edinburgh: Oliver and Boyd, 1978), 7.
[2] George Mackay Brown, *An Orkney Tapestry* (London: Gollancz, 1969), 20 and 50–51.

three generations Norday will be empty. For, says Progress, life in a city must be superior to life in an island....
Will there be a few folk left in the world, when Progress
is choked at last in its own too much? Yes, there will be.
A few folk will return by stealth to the wind and the mist
and the silences. I know it.[3]

This long preambulatory introduction to George
Mackay Brown and his oeuvre serves as a perfect introduction to his novel *Vinland*, published in 1992. As with his
earlier novel, *Magnus*, which was about the early twelfth-
century Earl of Orkney, St. Magnus the Martyr, *Vinland*
has as its inspirational and historical source the *Orkneyinga
Saga*, a Norse saga that tells of the history of the Orkneys
from the ninth to the thirteenth centuries. *Vinland* is set
in the late tenth and eleventh centuries, and, as the title
suggests, the story includes Leif Erikson's pioneering discovery of continental North America in around A.D. 1000,
almost half a millennium before the voyages of Christopher Columbus and John Cabot. It also includes the Battle
of Clontarf in Ireland, in which Viking forces under the
leadership of Sigurd of Orkney fought with an Irish army
led by Brian Boru.

Brown's depiction of the Vikings' first peaceful encounter with the Native Americans and their subsequent bloody
encounter with the native Irish is full of the evocative mys-
tique with which he approaches all reality. Nothing merely
happens in the literary world of George Mackay Brown;
everything is providential, the temporal always being kissed
or cursed by eternal powers, which make and break the
lives and ambitions of mortal men. This is all set as the

[3] George Mackay Brown, *Hawkfall and Other Stories* (London: The Hogarth
Press, 1974), 187.

backdrop of one man's life, Ranald Sigmundson, whose growth in wisdom and virtue, through the experience of often self-inflicted suffering, is the thread that weaves the mystic elements together into a unified wholesomeness.

In terms of time and space, *Vinland* resonates with the mystery of time and space itself. It is set at a time in which the old pagan deities and beliefs are being conquered by the new religion of the Christians, the latter of which offering the only hope for authentic human progress from the grip of barbarism; in terms of space, it is set in the mystic space in which the Old North meets the Mystic West, a space that fired the imagination of Tolkien, Lewis, and Sigrid Undset. The novel's concluding pages do not merely evoke this union of the Old North and the Mystic West but consummate it in the mysterious communion in which life and death meet in Christ. Few novels have ended so well in terms of good morals, true religion, and beautiful prose. If it is true that an artist can be defined "as a man who knows how to finish things", as Maurice Baring claimed, then the conclusion of *Vinland* proves that George Mackay Brown is a very fine artist indeed.

49

Declare

As we approach the end of this book in which we've endeavored to put great literature in a nutshell, an apology and an explanation are necessary. An apology is needed because the last two titles in this volume, this one and the next, are not truly canonical. They do not really belong in the canon of great books. This is due to the fact that they were published relatively recently and are by contemporary novelists. They have not stood the test of time.

In order to be "canonized", a book must have aged well, transcending the fads and fashions of the time in which it was written. Just as saints are not canonized until after they are dead, books should not be canonized until after their authors are dead. The author of *Declare* is very much alive (*Deo gratias!*) and is still writing good books. An explanation is therefore needed.

Tim Powers stands out from the crowd of contemporary novelists because he is a faithful Catholic who has somehow managed to swim in the toxic mainstream without compromising his faith or principles. This is a remarkable achievement in itself. It is not easy to make the *New York Times* Best Seller list without selling out to the demands and commands of the Zeitgeist.

Best known perhaps as the author of *On Stranger Tides*, which inspired *The Pirates of the Caribbean* films, his finest novel is probably or arguably *Declare*, a supernatural spy thriller set against the backdrop of World War Two and the Cold War.

Declare, as with much of Powers' work, is literary in the sense that it is awash with intertextual references to great literature. Its very title, as revealed in one of the three epigraphs that serve as curtain-raisers to the novel itself, is plucked from the Book of Job: *Where wast thou when I laid the foundations of the earth? Declare, if thou hast understanding.* The Prologue of the novel, which is set on Mount Ararat in 1948, begins with lines from *The Prelude* by Wordsworth; the opening chapter, which takes us to London in 1963, opens with lines of Edward Fitzgerald's translation of *The Rubaiyat* of Omar Khayyam; following chapters begin with literary snippets from Kipling's *Kim*, a work that recurs as a thematic motif as the story unfolds.

The deeper spiritual significance is suggested in the opening of another chapter with lines from Francis Thompson's "The Hound of Heaven", the theme of Thompson's poem echoing the providential "wyrdness" that is mystically present beneath the novel's natural surface and beyond the preternatural powers that lurk beneath its surface. The demonic dimension, the diabolical underbelly of the story, is voiced forth in another epigraph in the words of the serpent to Eve from the Book of Genesis. It is the devil's lying assurance that we "shall be as gods" if we forsake the path of humility and raise the flag of pride. This is the very temptation to which several of the characters succumb and is the very ethos of the Soviet spies who are seeking to harness the powers of darkness to win the world for the communist creed. The trouble is that those who seek to possess demonic power become possessed by it.

As for the key characters, the protagonist Andre Hale is a double agent, ostensibly in the service of the Soviets but in reality working for a mysterious British spy network, into which he had been initiated as a child by his devoutly Catholic mother, a former nun, immediately after receiving his first Holy Communion. The love interest is Elena, a young Spanish communist idealist who believes, mistakenly, that her parents had been killed by Franco's forces in the Spanish Civil War. She and Hale meet in Paris in 1941, while working for the French Resistance and for the Soviet Union as spies.

The antagonist is Kim Philby, a real-life Soviet spy, whom Powers places in the story to connect his historical fiction with history itself. This is a device that Powers employs in many of his works, introducing real historical characters into his fictional narratives to blend and blur fact with fiction, seducing the reader into the suggestion of realism in which we feel that we are entering history when we enter the story.

In terms of time, the story weaves from Hale's childhood in the years between the two world wars, to World War Two, and then to the cat-and-mouse espionage of the Cold War in the 1960s. In terms of space, it moves from London, Oxford, Paris, Berlin, Beirut, Kuwait, Mount Ararat, and finally to Moscow. Time and space are only the temporal and special surface on which the story moves; it is in what happens beneath the surface in the realm of preternatural powers that the novel reaches to the diabolical depths and the divine heights. It is a supernatural spy thriller akin to Chesterton's *The Man Who Was Thursday*, with which it bears some similarity, at least in terms of thematic kinship. It is apt, therefore, that the epigraph to the chapter that takes us into the demonic presence of the spirits lurking on Mount Ararat is taken from the dedicatory poem with which Chesterton begins his own supernatural spy thriller:

This is a tale of those old fears, even of those emptied
  hells,
And none but you shall understand the true things
  that it tells—
Of what colossal gods of shame could cow men and
  yet crash,
Of what huge devils hid the stars, yet fell at a pistol
  flash.[1]

This connection with Chesterton's novel, which was featured earlier, might be a good way to conclude our discussion of this more recent novel of a similar ilk. Is *Declare* destined to become as canonical as *The Man Who Was Thursday*? One should hesitate to "declare" one way or the other. It is not for the critic or the reader to play the prophet. As for this reader, I am certainly happy to declare without the least reservation or hesitation that *Declare* is well worth reading.

---

[1] G. K. Chesterton, "To Edmund Clerihew Bentley", in *The Man Who Was Thursday*, from the *Chesterton Omnibus* (London: Methuen, 1927).

50

Father Elijah

The penultimate "nutshell" in this book focused on *Declare* by Tim Powers, a Catholic writer who has succeeded in the secular culture without compromising his faith or his principles. In this final "nutshell", we will focus on *Father Elijah* by Michael D. O'Brien, a writer who has emerged as the most important voice in the literary cat-acombs, unknown to the toxic mainstream but widely read and greatly respected by those seeking the sort of solid Catholic literature that the secular culture has sought to "cancel".

Father Elijah, published in 1996, is Michael D. O'Brien's first and best-known novel. It tells the story of David Schäffer, a Jewish holocaust survivor who converts to Catholicism and subsequently becomes a Carmelite monk and priest. Father Elijah's efforts to combat the power of a charming and sinister world leader, who has all the hall-marks of being the Antichrist, invites comparisons with the plot of Robert Hugh Benson's *Lord of the World*. The obvious similarities aside, the most significant difference is that O'Brien doesn't set his novel in the distant future but at a time that is essentially contemporary. The ailing but holy and courageous pope bears a striking resemblance to John Paul II, and the fictional cardinal who is prefect for the Congregation of the Faith bears a remarkable resemblance to Joseph Ratzinger. This makes the apocalyptic twists and turns of the plot much closer to home than in Benson's futuristic apocalypse.

Surprisingly and paradoxically, O'Brien's contemporary setting has stood the test of time far better than Benson's futuristic dystopia. Benson had little option but to play the prophet, in a science-fiction sense, by inventing flying machines and other future-age technologies to make his setting seem realistic to his early twentieth-century readers. Today, in the real future, Benson's imaginatively fanciful future seems quaint and antiquated, at best, or, at worst, simply silly. By comparison, O'Brien's late twentieth-century setting seems enduringly contemporary. We can still imagine an ailing but courageous pope and equally courageous cardinals, as well as corrupt and theologically modernist members of the curia who are in league with the diabolical spirit of the world.

One of the particular strengths of *Father Elijah* is the way in which O'Brien brings his eponymous hero to fully fledged and fully fleshed life. He is not merely human, in the abstract sense, but a solid, concretely real person. We are moved by his dignity and doubt and are as troubled by his weaknesses as we are moved by them. We see him as a Jewish boy in Nazi-occupied Warsaw who is hidden from the authorities before making his escape. We are as haunted as he is by his return to Warsaw as an aged Carmelite monk. We are moved by the discoveries he makes and are disgusted by the diabolical evil that is uncovered.

Another strength of the book is the depiction of the deathbed conversion of an aging and decrepit débauché, whose past is poured forth to Father Elijah's disgust and discomfort and yet transformed by the holy priest's charity in the presence of a miserable sinner on the threshold of the abyss of death.

A further paradoxical strength of the novel is its handling of the protagonist's weakness. Before his conversion and calling to the priesthood and religious life, Father Elijah's pregnant wife had been killed in a terrorist bombing. The loss of his wife and unborn child leaves lasting scars, beyond healing, prompting the radical turn to Christ in conversion, reminding us of the immortal lines of Oscar Wilde about the potentially positive and life-changing power of suffering: "How else but through a broken heart may Lord Christ enter in."[1]

Later, when Father Elijah meets a beautiful widow, whose own husband had been murdered brutally by the sinister and diabolical forces that he is called to confront, he finds himself falling in love with her. This powerful temptation, a longing that could compromise his belonging to the Bride of Christ, is handled with great tact and dexterity by the author, the mark of a truly gifted storyteller. Such a gift is also present in the manner in which the supernatural penetrates the story. The presence of miraculous light demands a lightness of touch on the part of the author, the absence of which has ruined many a Christian novel through the clunkily inept handling of the deus ex machina. O'Brien also succeeds, for the most part, in avoiding the descent into preachiness, a fatal flaw that kills so much Christian literature with the kiss of deadly didacticism. That being said, the excision of a few pages of gratuitous spiritual musings would have exorcised the didactic spirit on the rare occasions when it emerges.

Michael D. O'Brien has written many other fine novels, several of which would have warranted a place in the present company of fifty great works of literature. Since, however, one must come to an end, we will allow his first novel to have the last word as the final "nutshell".

---

[1] Oscar Wilde, "The Ballad of Reading Gaol", Part V.

A DISCLAIMER AND FINAL WISH

It would seem appropriate that this volume should end with a disclaimer. Its author makes no claim that his selection of these particular books represents a definitive last word on what constitutes the literary classics. Quite the contrary. The fifty literary classics selected are but a small sampling of the numerous others that could have been included. Many will be perplexed by the exclusion of some of the truly great classics and will be puzzled by the inclusion of lesser-known works. If an apology is necessary, in addition to the disclaimer, it is offered here and now, and heartily.

Having made the disclaimer and apology, we will end with a final wish that these brief commentaries will serve as appetizers, offering a foretaste of what readers might expect when they delve and dive deeper into classic literature, whetting the appetite for more. If this slim volume inspires the reading of the classic works themselves, the wish will be granted and the author's labors will be richly rewarded.